D0319984

Beyond
Good Intentions

Beyond Good Intentions

A Mother Reflects on Raising
Internationally Adopted Children

CHERI REGISTER

Yeong & Yeong Book Company
St. Paul, Minnesota

Yeong & Yeong Book Company
St. Paul, Minnesota

©2005 by Cheri Register
All rights reserved. This book, or parts thereof, may not be
reproduced in any form without permission.

ISBN 978-1-59743-000-5

Cover design by Kim Dalros and Laurie Ingram
Interior design by Stephanie Billecke

Library of Congress Cataloging-in-Publication Data
Register, Cheri, 1945–
   Beyond good intentions : a mother reflects on raising
internationally adopted children / Cheri Register.
      p. cm.
   ISBN 1-59743-000-5 (alk. paper)
 1. Intercountry adoption. 2. Adoptees. I. Title.
   HV875.5.R44 2005
   362.734--dc22
                                        2005005409

Manufactured in Canada
12 11 10 09 08 07   2 3 4 5 6 7 8

To all who long for the love and security of family

Contents

Introduction

I am the American mother of two adult daughters adopted from Korea in infancy. Born in 1980 and 1983, on the upswing toward the peak of Korean adoption in 1985, they belong to a growing cohort of adult adoptees that also includes the children of the 1975 Vietnam Babylift and early adoptees from India, Colombia, the Philippines, and several other countries. Soon enough, before their parents know it, children from China, Russia, Ukraine, Kazakhstan, and elsewhere will enter adulthood. Our kids make up the largest and longest migration of homeless, orphaned, and relinquished children in history, a social experiment yet to be fully evaluated. Research is, of course, under way, and personal reflections on growing up adopted in Europe, the United Kingdom, Australia, Canada, and the United States are finding their way to print and to the screen. We parents can expect a vital learning experience.

As the mother of adults, I enjoy a retrospective view of adoptive child raising, having survived their toddlerhoods and teenage years and either avoided or extricated myself from many pitfalls, some created by my own ignorance. I am on good enough terms with my daughters to feel that our family life has been successful, at least by the measures that matter to me. We suffer no more strains than the average family. My older daughter currently lives in Korea, where she has met many other returning adoptees, some estranged from their parents and others critical of the way they were raised. Her e-mails relay what she has heard from these new friends and compare their families' habits with ours, prodding me to reflect on my behavior as a parent. I feel a sense of wonder that, in spite of all the risks inherent in international adoption, we have arrived at her adulthood with a sound relationship.

While she has been getting acquainted with adoptees from the United States, Denmark, Norway, Sweden, Switzerland, France, Italy, the Netherlands, Belgium, and Germany, I too have been listening to the voices of adult adoptees. They testify to the strengths and faults of adoptive family life on Internet lists and websites, at conferences on international adoption, and in poetry, memoirs, and documentary films. Their voices are on the leading edge of adoption literature, claiming the fertile ground where new truths arise to squeeze out the old, tired ones. Many of the voices are critical, and some of the testimony is difficult for parents to hear. Sometimes this listening has the furtive quality of eavesdropping. The adoptees are not always talking to or about us, but about themselves and their own present needs. They have more to gain from talking to each other and building community than from arguing with adoptive parents, either their own or the collective bunch of us.

Nevertheless, we parents are eager to join the conversation, and we are accustomed to setting the terms. I watched this happen at the publication reading of Jane Jeong Trenka's memoir, *The Language of Blood,* at the Loft Literary Center in Minneapolis in September 2003. The adoptees in the audience affirmed Trenka's account of her childhood in rural Minnesota and her reunion with her Korean birth family; they added their own stories, which were sometimes halted in mid sentence by tears. Some of the adoptive parents seemed perplexed and distressed by this emotional intensity. They homed their questions in on the reasons for it and even tried to explain it away.

An earnest couple, prospective parents waiting for a child from Guatemala, asked what they could do differently to make life turn out well for their own child so she would not end up sad or angry—in other words, like Jane and the adoptees in the audience.

As a memoirist myself, I am mindful that readers cull personal stories for general advice and even measure the legitimacy of the personal account against what they already believe to be true. As a mother, I sensed Jane's discomfort at having not just her literary effort but her life itself laid open for scrutiny and analysis. I wanted to rush in and save her, but resisted the impulse until I had one clear comment to offer. We need to remember that adoptees are as unique and diverse as any other population. If we listen intently to their testimony, we curious parents can begin to discern patterns that will answer our questions. That's more considerate than asking adoptees to plumb their pain for foolproof advice.

Those who examine the abandonment and displacement that have shaped their lives owe us parents neither congratulations nor apologies nor explanations. It is not their duty to rescue us from our mistakes or to relieve the

Cheri Register

discomfort we feel when they are unhappy. Listening is crucial, but we parents must also talk to each other. There are, of course, organizations and publications and Internet sites where adoptive parents share their joys and seek mutual help in times of trouble. But nearly all of these are dominated by parents of young children. As our children begin to hone their interests and choose their friends and resist adoption-related activities, we parents pull away into our separate social spheres. Forums intended for parents of adult adoptees are not easy to find. I feel lucky to be one of "The Moms," a small, informal group of mothers of Korean-born teenagers and adults that meets biweekly for breakfast.

As an experienced parent, I can address the weighty question that the parents-to-be asked Jane Jeong Trenka: What should we do differently? Because I have heard so much pain in the adoptees' voices, the advice has come to me in shadow form, the obverse of the upbeat, foolproof guide to correct parenting that new parents long for. There is no foolproof way to raise children, especially children uprooted from their original families and cultures. The risks are tremendous, and it is the risks I have chosen to present: *ten pitfalls that adoptive parents can easily slip into, with unfortunate consequences for their children and their family relationships.*

Each chapter opens with an exaggerated version—a caricature—of something an adoptive parent might say. If you think you recognize yourself, be assured my voice is there, too. The point of a caricature is not to demean, but to prompt a fresh look at features so familiar we no longer notice them. I use exaggeration to home in on some conventional wisdom I want to re-examine, drawing on lessons distilled from reading and listening to others and on my experience as a well-meaning but fallible parent. International adoption is a vast, unprecedented social experiment with still uncertain conclusions. We parents who undertake it all intend to do our best, yet we risk stumbling over our good intentions and tumbling into pitfalls of misunderstanding and ignorance. Although you may not agree with everything I say, I hope you will join me in a candid discussion of our common challenge: how to do right by our kids.

Because I focus on the extremes at each end of a range of behavior, you may feel damned if you do and damned if you don't. I urge you to remember that the wisest course is often through the middle, the "happy medium" between the extremes. Raising children, adopted or not, requires us to steer our families safely through the roiling waters between the Charybdis of tyranny and the Scylla of neglect. It's a tough, scary, and sometimes unforgiving job. Yet it is also joyous and rewarding.

My natural inclination is to tell my own story in the style of memoir or personal essay, to investigate it in full detail, and to draw out the lessons that come with hindsight. This is what I normally do as a writer, when the subject matter is some critical aspect of my own life. In this case, however, telling my story fully would mean exposing my daughters' private lives as well. One lesson I have learned that I am eager to pass on to readers is that our children's experience of being adopted internationally is their exclusive property, theirs to tell or not, theirs to interpret. I have chosen not to spell out details that would put my daughters on the spot or incite strangers to ask them probing personal questions. My passion for writing about this tender subject must not cause them pain. Yet I assure readers that all of my generalizations arise out of specific incidents I have read or observed or been told, a few of them my own bumbling attempts to do right by my family.

I set out to address a broad audience of parents adopting from all the "sending" countries. The problem of how to be inclusive without cluttering the prose with country names stumped me at first. I tried familiar fictional places— Freedonia, Shangri-La, Brigadoon—but those were already loaded with meaning. Then I remembered a lecture I heard my first week of college about the strange habits of the Nacirema. We green freshmen dutifully took notes until, one by one, we got the joke. If you turn *adopt* backwards, you get *tpoda,* which could pass as the name of a country and is easily anglicized as *Tapoda.* Suppose Tapoda fell on hard economic times or went through a rapid, socially disruptive industrialization and urbanization or instituted a punitive population control policy. How might the Tapodans cope with rising numbers of homeless children? Tapoda will be the code word for whatever country you, the reader, may have adopted from. Alternating the gender of pronouns will solve another problem. Because I have an academic background in Scandinavian languages and

Cheri Register

can also read German, Dutch, and French, I have searched the Internet for accounts of adoptive families in Europe and read some publications in those languages, including adoptee memoirs. Though I have tried to make my discussion relevant to all the adopting countries, my vantage point is still the United States, specifically Minnesota, the state with the highest number of Korean adoptees per capita. "Are you from anywhere other than Minnesota?" American adoptees in Seoul ask each other.

At the time I adopted my children, all the sending countries I knew of were in Asia and Latin America. After the dissolution of the Soviet Union in 1991, Russian orphanages became a popular new source of adoptable children. The parents of Eastern European children perceive them as white and thus free of the complications involved in transracial adoption. This comforting perception may be illusory. Given the volatile history of this part of the world and the prospect of rising nationalisms and ethnic conflicts, ethnicity might become a critical matter for these adoptees.

One promising trend is a growing interest in adoption among the children and grandchildren of immigrants from the sending countries. Among the parents in the United States adopting from China, for example, are many Chinese Americans. Singapore, home to many ethnic Chinese, is experiencing a decline in birthrate and has opened channels for adoption from China. Some adoptees have adopted from their birth countries in addition to bearing children. These families will likely have their own practiced means of dealing with racial issues, and they will match well enough to be spared rude stares and questions. When I talk about race, I am indeed addressing white parents. What I say here about loss, grief, personal identity, and birth heritage, however, applies to all adoptive families. I invite readers to select what is useful to you, and I wish you a smooth journey through calm waters.

Finally, I must acknowledge that I am wary of the growing popularity of international adoption. In the United States, for example, the number of visas granted to children arriving for adoption increased more than 250 percent in a single decade, from 1990 to 2000. What many of us saw as a temporary child welfare measure has become a self-perpetuating exchange, an important source of revenue in some poor countries, and a safety valve that delays social reform. Rather than serving would-be parents' needs as supply-and-demand dictates, international adoption should be governed by a concern for children that puts greater emphasis on keeping families intact and daily life sustainable in the countries where they are born.

This view is not incompatible with my love for my daughters. Imagine that you are looking at the world through a telephoto lens. Up close, you are charmed by the smiles of little children cuddled in the arms of beaming adoptive parents. Many of us prefer to keep the focus that tight. If you dial back for the long view, however, you see poverty, injustice, and the sorrow of parents who must relinquish their children to keep them alive and healthy or to avoid stigma or punishment. Everything you see, whether close or distant, is really there. The joy and the tragedy coexist. That is the paradox of adoption, and we are all caught up in it. Your family's cohesion over the long haul depends on how you come to terms with that paradox.

1

Wiping Away Our Children's Past

I am so thrilled to be adopting a baby from Tapoda. Finally, I'm going to have the son I've always dreamed of, and I'll treat him exactly as if he were born to me. I can't imagine loving my "own" child any more than I love this little guy already. Adoption is a perfectly fine way to create a family, and now that it's done, we'll just be a normal family like any other. The fact that he's adopted shouldn't make any difference. We are his real parents now, and he's all ours.

In the early days of international adoption, after the Korean War in the 1950s and up through the 1970s, the guiding wisdom was to help the children assimilate into their new families and communities. Parents of domestically adopted children whose histories were kept secret, locked away in social service agency files, received the same advice. Babies were blank slates just waiting for a new family to inscribe its habits and values. Even older children could be scrubbed clean and given a fresh start with brand new identities. The past no longer mattered, and children showed a remarkable capacity to forget unpleasant events.

In the meantime, we've learned a great deal about human genetics that contradicts that advice. Children are not blank slates, but more like blueprints, with certain temperaments and tendencies all sketched in place. A path-breaking study of twins raised apart, conducted by the Minnesota Center for Twin and Family Research at the University of Minnesota, found that the twins often eat the same snacks, have the same taste in music, take up the same hobbies—in short, exhibit shared traits previously thought to be learned. A child separated from his birth family preserves much of the genetic heritage bred into that family, which, for all we don't know, may have taken root in Tapoda after the last great migration eight hundred years ago. He shares no genes with his adoptive parents, though he will likely mimic many of their gestures and—they hope, anyway—absorb their beliefs and values.

We've also learned more about the human brain: repressing the memory of a traumatic event is not the same as forgetting. Many parents who adopt older children would like to rewind the tragic past and tape happier memories in its place. They find it hard to believe that a child mistreated or abused by his parents, for example, may yet feel some residue of love for them. A child from a war-torn or impoverished country may see beauty in places that make his parents recoil. I hope never to forget the way a fourteen-year-old boy whom I interviewed for my book *"Are Those Kids Yours?"* described his former home in Colombia, where he had spent the first half of his life. The rich detail with which he evoked the landscape suggested an artistic sensibility that needed memory to thrive and be put to use. His parents constantly urged him to forget the past and look ahead. They were afraid he would get nostalgic about Colombia and glamorize it. But nostalgia, literally *ache to return,* is no trivial emotion. Our memories of the past are the raw material from which we construct ourselves and the stories of our lives.

Desire for a family with whom we feel total affinity is a fundamental human longing. How ready I was to believe my sister's taunts that my parents had found me on the doorstep and kept me only because the police said they had to. That story could have made sense of all the ways in which I felt like an oddball in my family, if I hadn't had my mother's skinny nose and scant chin. Still, I had fantasies of another family somewhere in the world that shared my every quirk. An adopted child who feels like an oddball *does* have another family, and no semantic games about who is the "real" parent will quell his curiosity about, or longing for, people who resemble him. Even if he doesn't articulate the longing, it may lurk as a vague uneasiness, a sense of displacement. If strangers can tell just by looking that he doesn't quite belong to your family, some will certainly be rude enough to ask for explanations. When you rush to make light of the difference or act embarrassed to have it acknowledged, he may conclude that you are ashamed of it—and of him. To ward off the shame, he assumes a false sense of self that doesn't correspond with how he looks. A glimpse of himself in the mirror is startling because he doesn't expect to see a Tapodan.

Denying a child's genetic heritage and hush-hushing his original family amount to stealing his birthright, all that he brought with him into the world, including his potential to become his best self. Over the years since I adopted my daughters, the word in use as the correct, neutral term for the women who bore them—*birth mother*—has become more and more distasteful to me. I haven't found any better replacement, but I am troubled by its connotations. *Birth mother* sounds too functional; it suggests to me a brood mare or an egg-laying hen. *Birth father,* by contrast, stands for a person too seldom acknowledged. Their parents gave my children so much more than birth: their beauty, their temperaments, their voices, their wits. I have contributed plenty myself: unconditional love, affectionate discipline, education and encouragement, whatever values I managed to convey, my troublesome

Scandinavian habits of indirection. . . . When I look at my adult daughters now, I do see the chips off my block, but I am more and more curious about how they reflect the features of their unknown parents, especially now that they have reached and passed the ages their mothers were when they were born.

The word *entitlement* is often brandished in adoption circles as a prerequisite to bonding with our children. To be an effective parent and to achieve a healthy family relationship, you must, the experts urge, never doubt the legitimacy of your claim to your child. This is important advice, but it can be misleading. When you marry, you "cleave unto" your spouse and sever all other romantic ties. Bigamy, in Western cultures, is both immoral and illegal. Despite the legal separation and transfer of parental rights that take place in adoption, your child is capable of loving you and still having intense feelings about those other parents off in the distance. It's natural for him to wonder about the source of his traits and behaviors, the source of his life itself. This curiosity, even when it evolves into longing and then into searching, doesn't negate the value of your parenthood or diminish your importance in your child's life. It's not rejection, not disloyalty. *It is not even about you.*

In most of the adopting countries, even parents whose children were born to them are expected to ease up on their claims at some point, to "let go" and trust the children to take up adulthood on their own terms. Your letting go may send your child farther afield, to an ethnic culture other than your own, to another city or region where he doesn't always have to explain himself, even back to Tapoda and to his original family. Although a minority of international adoptees actually searches for birth parents, those who do search feel driven by a primal need. As Christina Nagel, a Chilean Dane writing in *Budstikken,* the newsletter of Foreningen for Adopterede, phrases it, "The best way I can get people to understand my/our situation is when I say, 'I have a hole inside, and that hole was made when I was adopted away. The cork for that hole is in the hands of my biological parents.' Now the question is only—do I dare find that cork?" Your inclination, as the older, wiser being, may be to prepare your child for disappointment by warning that psychic holes aren't so easily and swiftly filled. Yet if you love your child and truly want what's best for him, you will cheer him on in his quest for a familial and cultural history. And he will love you back. If you set yourself up in competition with your child's other parents, you will likely lose.

If you wipe away that other family, you not only hurt your children, but also limit yourself. You give in to your baser instincts—fear and jealousy, especially. Some parents admit that they chose international adoption thinking the extra distance reduced the threat that the mother would come and reclaim her child. Many of us cluck self-righteously about parents who say such things, but every one of us has at least a tiny insecurity gurgling inside. Whatever made us think that this child, plucked out of Tapoda and plopped into our alien family, would actually love and be loyal to us? I often imagine the two women to whom I owe my life's greatest joy. I would never begrudge them or my/their daughters the right to know and love each other. But I can say that confidently only because my resolve has not yet been tested.

The majority of parents adopting now come to adoption out of personal misfortune: an inability to conceive the children they expected to bring into the world. It's natural to feel jealous of people who conceive accidentally or without forethought and even to turn that jealousy into disdain for those who don't accept the consequences. Desire alone, some argue, makes the infertile prospective parent more suited to raise the child and thus more deserving, more entitled. If you enter adoption with disdain, or even just pity, for your child's parents, you may think you are doing him a favor by protecting him from reminders of those unworthy or pitiful people.

As long as the birth parents' whereabouts are unknown, we adoptive parents wield the awesome power to create them for our children. This realization hit home for me when I read Susan Tompkins's account, in the anthology *A Passage to the Heart,* of a talk she had with her thirteen-year-old daughter: "I spoke of how much I cared about her birth mother, how beautiful and smart she must be, how sad her life must be, and, of course, what an incredible gift she gave us." My feelings resonated with her deep concern for the birth mother's loss, but "how sad her life must be" rang off key. Does our children's self-esteem depend on imagining their birth mothers as perennially sad, incapable of restoring joy to their lives, or as so self-demeaning they will offer a child as a "gift" to other (more deserving?) parents? That's better, I suppose, than portraying them as wanton or careless or neglectful. Or is it? Mirim Kim, a Korean American adoptee, raised this question in a poem written in the voice of a birth mother who pleads, "have your fantasies in your own space / I resent being forced—pressured to—play the role / of the loving despairing mother / I never wanted to be." Her point, she explained to me in an e-mail, was to assert her right to feel a range of emotions toward her mother, not just the approved sorrow and gratitude. At the same time, she freed her unknown birth mother of the reigning mystique and let her be real. When we parents try to portray our children's birth parents out of scant evidence, maybe we *are* robbing them of their reality, bringing them under our imaginative control, and reducing their threat to us. A wiser option is to be truthful about what little we know.

Mixed in with any jealousy and fear infertile parents might feel is grief for the missing flesh-and-blood offspring. If you have entertained dreams of that child, conjured him up and imagined nursing him, pushing him through the park in his stroller, taking him to kindergarten, reading his splendid report cards, cheering at his Little League home runs, beaming through his valedictory speech . . . then those dreams have left expectations in their wake. You want to believe that loving your adopted child enough and making him all your own will fulfill those expectations. To seal the deal, you replace his Tapodan name with the precious baby name held in reserve through the long years of infertility and baptize him in all your best hopes for that baby. He has, in effect, become a substitute child.

A substitute life is dangerous territory for an adopted child to crawl through. He is not equipped with the requisite genetic material to follow your design. He's not genetically inferior; he just has the wrong wiring for the uses to which you want to put him. You want him to be the life of the party, like you are, but he's quiet and contemplative, or vice versa. He's likely to fail you. If you don't admit to your disappointed hopes for your "own" baby, who may never have lived up to your fantasy either, that disappointment will wash over the child you have, and you will overlook the treasures he offers you. He is not a blank slate, not a substitute child, but a uniquely promising human being with traits that will surprise and delight you if you give him room to flourish. Those traits were passed on to him by a long line of Tapodans who deserve your respect and gratitude. He may well be curious about the source of those traits. When Camilla Pedersen, a Korean Norwegian adoptee appearing in *Korean Quarterly,* realized she had a talent for writing, she began to wonder, "Was my birth mother a writer? My father? Did I have an unknown, famous writing brother or sister in Korea?"

My first daughter was a verbal child who quickly learned to put sentences together. I had been too, and my family frequently joked that it was all in our genes. I took pride in this and felt my expectations rise. With my guidance, her childhood could be a new, improved version of my own. I managed to back off—at least I think I did—thanks to my second child. She arrived with a budding personality quite unlike her sister's. Words came slowly, and she compensated by making up her own clever names for the objects around her. Movies, not books, are her medium, and she quotes dialogue and cites visual cues long afterward as though she expects the rest of us to get the allusion. This child had clearly been outfitted from some other trove of genetic gems than any my birth family ever lucked upon.

Motherhood's first big thrill was watching my children reveal their personalities. Ten months and four months at arrival, they were already people in their own right. They were not mine to mold and mess up, but arrived with distinct characters that would prevail as long as they didn't get squelched. This was a humbling, but also a liberating, discovery. Motherhood seemed less grandiose than I had imagined, but more manageable. If I backed up a little and watched these wonderful people emerge, my role in their emergence would be less burdensome for all of us. As delightful as my daughters have been from the beginning—ignoring for now the inevitable exasperations—I often wonder about the ancestors who made them this way.

My daughters wonder too, and from time to time they have talked about it. Another surprise is how much children's curiosity about genetic family fluctuates. The nature and intensity of these feelings vary with age and stage, and from child to child, consistent with other traits of character. I have learned to regard this as private territory, to be ready to listen when the feelings are voiced and to comfort if need be. My daughters know that if they search for their Korean families, I will participate in whatever way they invite me to. Still, the prospect of meeting their families scares me a little. I expect we will all be trembling some.

My route to family life did not veer through the trials of infertility. My fertility has never been tested because my desire from the outset was to avoid pregnancy. I was diagnosed at nineteen with a chronic illness that could endanger both mother and child if I were to conceive. If I wanted children, the doctors told me, I would be wise to adopt them, and even then my life span might not be sufficient to raise them. Also, I came of age at a time when family and career were thought incompatible for women, and my enrollment at the University of Chicago seemed a clear enough statement of which I was fit for.

Yet like most little girls of my pre-Barbie generation, I had played at motherhood and cuddled and dressed a family of dolls that grew by one each Christmas. I imagined myself someday choosing between two destinies: either writing books in a Northwoods hermitage or raising four-teen children in a spacious Victorian house. I had fourteen names picked out and fourteen personalities to go with them. When I recall them now, they seem like fictional characters, offspring of the mind, not the womb.

By the time my husband and I decided to adopt, in our thirties, I had already shed the typical hopes and dreams. (He hadn't, but that's another story, not mine to tell.) Because I had never seriously expected children, adoption felt like a bonus, an undeserved reward for out-living my life expectancy. Although I join the chorus that asks infertile parents to grieve their losses before adopt-ing, I haven't done that grieving because I haven't yet felt the need. In that way, I resemble adoptees who feel no need to grieve the loss of birth family or who find other coping skills, which may be what I, in my fundamental optimism, have done.

Maybe the grief is yet to come. I've heard that cer-tain life passages can call forth old, unexpressed grief. I didn't feel grief at divorce about not bearing children, but instead felt anxious about losing the children I had until custody was settled. At menopause I felt some qualms about aging, but not about missing out on reproduction. When my daughters left home for college, it was them I missed, not my unborn biological heirs. And when my parents died, I had no regrets about not passing along their genes. My sisters had seen to that. Maybe I will grieve if and when my daughters find and form relationships with their birth families, especially if they leave me out. Maybe I will grieve if and when my daughters have children. Pregnancy and the birth of a grandchild have proven to be sensitive times in some adoptive families because they bring back the infertile parents' feelings of failure and loss. The child's resemblance to her parents, no matter how pleasing, may also be a sad reminder that the grandparents have no genetic connection. The new parent may be struck by that as well. A Danish adoptee writes on an Internet forum, "I have to admit, no matter how controversial or ungrateful some people will see it, that I feel like my family is starting now with me. I am point zero, and not a continuation of my adoptive parents' families." Holding a new child can be a painful reminder that the grandparents missed the early weeks or months or years of their own children's lives. Memories of filling bottles with soy formula may pale at the sight of a nursing mother establishing that primal physical bond with her child. Maybe I will grieve if my daughters don't have children. I do have expectations of a glorious grandmahood, whether by birth or by adoption.

2

Hovering over Our "Troubled" Children

I do my best to monitor my daughter's feelings because I know that the primal wound of separation has left her emotionally fragile. When she's unhappy, I make sure to mention her birth mother, because she is undoubtedly thinking about her. I watch her like a hawk for signs of trauma. If she starts to act up in the critical preadolescent years, I'll make sure we get those adoption issues out in the open before they erupt and turn her into a teenage volcano. I worry that if she doesn't come to terms with her grief, she'll never be able to manage life on her own.

The popular wisdom on adoption swings like a pendulum between two extremes. One pole is the conviction that being adopted is of no more consequence than being born into your family. The other is the belief that the separation or loss that precedes adoption is so traumatic that it damages the child forever. Psychologists' warnings about "adoption syndrome" helped bring secret domestic adoptions out of the closet and made advocates of international adoption encourage parents to drop the pretense of assimilation. No matter how you acquire your children, it's all, as seasoned parents will tell you, a crapshoot.

Still, there are more unknowns to contend with in the case of adoption. To seize control in the face of uncertainty, some parents focus on the single fact they do know for sure: that their children have been severed from their roots. As long as they keep this initial trauma foremost in mind, they believe, they are less likely to be swept off guard by its turbulent consequences. Some parents simply keep their seismographs turned on, while others treat every little tremor as a sign that the big quake is on the way.

Many children do arrive in their new homes with serious physical, emotional, and cognitive impairments.

These problems are especially common in those who come from orphanages ill-equipped to offer the large numbers of children they house the foundation for a healthy life. Children show up malnourished, diseased, or marked by skin disorders that hygiene easily available in the adopting countries could have prevented. They arrive with hardly any language and without the prewiring for language that babies acquire simply by being talked to. These problems need quick attention and consistent long-term treatment. The parents of these children share common ground with parents who give birth to physically and developmentally disabled children, though the adoptive parents may hold greater hopes for their children's recovery.

In any population of children, certain impairments go undetected at first or don't manifest until later on. Some adoptees' lives will be dogged by serious disorders, including hereditary ones for which there is no documented history. These, too, will require ongoing parental vigilance. What I say from here on refers to adoptees who are primarily healthy, not those with disabilities so severe that they have little hope of living independently in adulthood.

Even the bouncing babies tended by indulgent foster parents pay a psychological price for their adoption. Being lifted out of a foster mother's arms is a second abandonment, and being greeted by a smiling, tear-stained face of a color and shape never seen before has got to be scary. Korean American Katy Robinson, in her memoir *A Single, Square Picture,* recalls her first impression, at age seven, of her adoptive parents: "I saw them in the distance—two foreigners who looked as strange as monsters. The woman had a long pointy nose, white skin splashed with tiny brown spots, orange hair and pale green eyes. The man had only a few strands of long silvery hair brushed across his shiny head, while large bushy clumps of hair hung from his chin like a lion."

If this is how an intelligent seven-year-old sees us, imagine how we look to a baby or toddler who has not yet learned to distinguish humans from other creatures. Some of us older parents remember the forlorn sounds our new babies made when they cried. At the time, we identified that sound as the child's unique crying voice, but now, having listened with trained ears to other crying babies, we're inclined to read meaning in that mournful cry. It's fair to assume that even a healthy child has undergone a trauma or two by the time you begin celebrating her presence in your family. A deep-seated grief and fear of abandonment are endemic among adoptees, and they are likely to surface at some time in life, especially when prodded loose by other disturbances, such as divorce or death in the family, new siblings, moves or other disruptions in the routine, and adolescent hormonal change.

As I walk through my gentrifying neighborhood, I often meet younger adoptive parents beaming over cute little kids tucked into padded and shaded state-of-the-art strollers. I smile back knowingly, but don't dare say what I'm thinking: Don't be surprised if your daughter shoplifts, or slips into a deep depression, or flies into a rage and threatens you with a knife before falling into a sobbing heap on the floor. Don't be surprised if your son fires obscenities at you, or skips his classes senior year and barely graduates, or fails to come home several nights in a row and then blames his absence on your inhospitality. Adolescence is a volatile time anyway, and it is common for teenage adoptees to tend toward the extremes of rage, on the one hand, and self-loathing, on the other.

These new parents probably wouldn't hear me. My hearing was more selective back then too. I wrote *"Are Those Kids Yours?"* while my kids were at one of life's most pleasant, affectionate stages, the primary grades of elementary school. I interviewed a fourteen-year-old girl, known as Amy Andrews in the book, who confessed to feeling such terrible rage at twelve and thirteen that she had even threatened her parents with a knife. It was an alarming story and, I thought, pretty bizarre. I down-played it in the book, with only a mention of "the rage that had made her lash out at her parents, withdraw from her friends, and feel miserable herself." If I were to write the book again, I would give it more credence and more space on the page. I've heard enough testimony now to understand that it's not bizarre. Alarming, yes, but not bizarre. My purpose in telling it would not be to frighten those new parents, but simply to pull the romantic cotton from their ears. And then I would add: Be prepared, but don't hover in anticipation or you will surely drive your child and yourselves to the brink.

The trick we parents need to master is to see the uprooting as traumatic without pathologizing the child as damaged, a hapless victim perennially incapable of caring for herself. That troubling behavior is a fairly normal adolescent response to an abnormal circumstance. Yes, adoption is a fine way to form a family. Yes, family life is generally better than orphanage care. Yes, adoption saves children from homelessness, disability, and even death. But it is not ideal or trouble-free. Being separated from family and displaced at a tender age to a foreign culture, where sights, sounds, smells, tastes are vastly different, *is* an abnormal circumstance. So is growing up in a family of another race than your own in a setting where your race defines you as exotic or inferior. Adapting to abnormal circumstances takes effort at any age. The emotional part of that effort is beyond a child's understanding. Even the facts of adoption are confusing. Feelings emerge with stunning power before the capacity to make rational sense of them develops. Long-simmering grief can erupt as anger. Fueled by surging hormones, anger lets loose as rage or gets subdued into depression. Grief has few proper, safe outlets. Even people who simply cry it out are likely to be cast as troubled if they don't quickly dry their tears and get back to business. Grief can as easily take expression, or seek comfort, in shoplifting, promiscuous sex, eating disorders, self-mutilation, violence, or drug abuse—behaviors readily available anyway to youth in Western countries.

Nearly all adoptive families encounter times of crisis that could be eased by therapy. The purpose of skilled and knowledgeable therapy is not to "fix" the child, but to help the whole family reveal unspoken feelings, understand where they come from, and learn nondestructive ways to release them. Therapists familiar with what Dee Paddock, in her "Families with a Difference" web pages, calls "normal and predictable issues in adoptive family life" will know best how to treat your child without stigmatizing her. They will recognize that she is just trying mightily to pull her genuine, healthy self out from under an abnormal load of stress. And they will help you become what Paddock calls a *proactive parent,* one who lives in a calm and understanding state of readiness, rather than a *reactive parent* who panics and pounces. "Effective therapists," Paddock writes, "acknowledge the impact of adoption on families while honoring the reality that we can't focus on adoption as the only defining aspect of our family."

The bold testimony of adult adoptees who describe the rough times they have been through scares some parents into a neurosis of control. Not *my* child, they insist, and they rev up their psychic vacuum cleaners, determined to clean out the festering residue of adoption trauma and send it off to the lab to be diagnosed. Their refuge is a medical model that matches prescribed treatment to precisely identified problems. They miss the other, vitally important message in the adult adoptees' testimony: We are not weak and pitiful. We are healthy, normal human beings who have suffered and survived massive loss and dizzying confusion.

Indigo Williams, a Vietnamese Australian adoptee, told me in an email that she keeps a picture of Nelson Mandela on her refrigerator as a symbol of strength and survival. She suggests that adoptees, especially those who encounter racism, "need to seek a range of people to both validate our experiences, even the painful ones, and show how great our potential is." Rather than pity Mandela for the years he spent imprisoned on Robben Island, people admire him for using that time to refine his ideals and for putting them into practice once he was released. The trying times in adoptees' lives can be, like Mandela's imprisonment, crucibles of strength. We parents must stop short, however, of holding our kids accountable for Mandela-level achievements. There are fitting models among adoptees themselves.

One of those survivors is "Amy Andrews," a mother herself now and a promising writer and scholar nearing thirty. The rageful teenager she once was has spawned sassy Asian American characters for young adult fiction. Her graduate research in cross-cultural psychology looks at how Asian cultures define mental health and how they perceive the rage she has seen in herself and other Korean adoptees. Those new parents in my neighborhood who, I expect, would close their ears to the knife episode may end up buying Amy's short stories for their children and drawing comfort from her research.

The only certain way to stave off the grief is to eliminate the cause. Instead of claiming the world's children as our own, we could support their birth families and communities and help them stay together. But the damage has already been done, you lament. You have a child who is a living pressure tank of adoption issues. She wants to sleep with you every night, but you've compromised at leaving her light on and sitting in her room until she falls asleep. She clings to you when you take her to preschool and won't let you out the door without awful pangs of guilt. She has separation anxiety, the teachers tell you, and the best treatment is to leave quickly, don't linger, and soon enough she'll see the pattern and trust you to come back each afternoon. You blame it on her separation from her birth mother, and you're probably right. So you ask her if she misses her birth mother and worries that you will leave her too. She's puzzled by the question, and this puzzles you. She hasn't been thinking about abandonment at all, yet the next day she clings to you and sobs just like the day before. This is so frustrating. If only she could see the connection and accept that you are her "forever" mommy or daddy, this separation anxiety would go away. How are you going to make this clingy four-year-old understand?

She doesn't understand; she only feels. As she gets older, you see new evidence that fears of abandonment have a hold on her life. She has difficulty making solid friends because she doesn't trust other kids to like her and be loyal to her. Going out of town, even when you're by her side, unsettles her and makes her crabby. She's a creature of habit who devises little rituals to mark the moments in her daily routine. If you move her stuff because it's cluttering your path, her temper flares. All of this, you are convinced, has to do with adoption. Indeed, much of it does, and sometimes pointing that out to her puts her at ease. It's when her blank stare tells you she just doesn't get it that you feel most frustrated and powerless. Once again, you probe her psyche with the wand of your vacuum. If you could only lift out each adoption issue and examine it closely, you could get the problem diagnosed and treated, but she refuses to cooperate. She's never in the right mood for the Big Talk about adoption that will bathe all her problems in the light of day. You're eager to deal with them, to preempt an eruption that could inundate the whole family, but she's in denial.

In an article in *Korean Quarterly* subtitled "The Rage of Adopted Koreans," adoptee Chad Potter Juncker asks, "How is an adoptee supposed to rationally communicate his or her feelings to someone if they don't know what they are going through in the first place? It's like a young child who has a severe eye problem and needs glasses.

How is the child supposed to know of a need for glasses? They have never seen the world any differently." We parents should pose a few questions to ourselves. How well do I understand myself? Have I identified all my own quirky behaviors and traced them to their original sources? How much self-awareness are human beings capable of at four or fourteen or forty?

Imagine a nonadoptive parent taking a young child aside and saying, "When you're thirteen or fourteen you're going to begin having feelings that make you uncomfortable and cranky and maybe even mad at me. So let's talk about it now and get it over with." Heading off adolescent turmoil before the hormones hit and the child has some clue about what you mean by "feelings" is pretty unlikely. To pick at adoption issues and expect your child to respond like a self-aware adult is equally unrealistic. To label her lack of response *denial* or *avoidance* or *arrested development* is presumptuous. And to regard your own inability to lay bare and control her feelings as a sign of *her* pathology can damage your relationship. Anyone who has experienced trauma will tell you there are realms of privacy that are best protected and to which others can be admitted only when there is genuine assurance of safety. That assurance of safety has to come, finally, from within. Your child will deal with her adoption issues when *she's* good and ready.

You are a loving parent, however, and you can't stand to watch her flounder, as wounded and fragile as you imagine her to be. She's probably not as helpless as you think, and neither are you. First, you can stay alert to *her* cues and listen when she chooses to talk. If you can listen without passing judgment or too quickly offering remedies and especially without getting upset, she may come to trust you and to feel safe exposing her feelings to you. Yet she is just as likely to erupt all over you and take her feelings out on you for the same reasons: because she trusts that you will still love her and not freak out and run away. Being the safe, reliable adult in her life has its costs and benefits. Just remember that she's a kid—not a damaged kid, but an immature kid who is still learning how to handle her troubling emotions and come to terms with her unusual history.

The best help you can offer your child is to shift your attention from her wounds to her strengths. There are times when the wounds need tending, and you and your child are both best served by experienced outside help. But don't let your expectations of trouble obscure the ordinary moments when life simply asks to be lived. At those moments, you can afford to love her unconditionally, nurture her gifts, indulge her interests, and surround her with a community of support. Human beings manage to survive trauma of all sorts and still lead reasonably happy lives. This capacity for survival is often called *resilience.* The familiar saying "Children are resilient" is not always welcome in adoption circles because it's easily misinterpreted to mean that children are impervious to harm. A term I have found useful is *ontological security,* one I latched onto back when R. D. Laing was a fixture in pop psychology. It refers to a trust in self, a worthy *I* who can be buffeted and pummeled by circumstance but still see value in living. This inner core of security doesn't develop easily in an atmosphere of fussy overprotectiveness unless the child has enough in-born gumption to rebel and fend it off.

The best help we can offer ourselves is to talk freely with other adoptive parents about what we and our children are going through. Between the glossy happily-ever-after adoption stories and the bad-seed horror tales is a nice, wide space for the woes and worries that are normal features of adoptive family life. While it's difficult to establish cause and effect—are adopted children more likely than birth children to end up in therapy because they need it more or because adoptive parents are more inclined to seek help?—the professionals' perception is that our families have more issues to deal with. When we talk to other adoptive parents about these issues, we find not only empathy, practical support for our efforts, and balm for our fear and guilt, but also a new consensus about what is *normal.*

I wish I could say I have been a mellow mom, never fretful, always quietly attuned to my daughters' emotional needs, but I would be lying. I too have had grandiose ambitions of sparing my daughters from pain and suffering through perceptive, loving vigilance. And I have, on occasion, been blindsided by the unexpected. "What do you know?" one of my teenage daughters once demanded. "You've never been adopted." I had just made some sweeping generalization meant to sweep trouble under the rug.

I repeat her line to myself often, even as I sit here and write from my limited capacity to understand.

I must admit, too, that my family has not endured the extremes of grief-induced behavior. We have known anger and depression. I have had bedroom doors slammed in my face and heard my share of yelled "I hate you"s. I have yelled back and taken myself for drives around the neighborhood to restore my composure. We have been to therapy and have learned the importance of serotonin to our everyday well-being. But we have never yet needed police intervention, hospitalization, or out-of-home placement. I know families who have experienced these things. I drink coffee with the mothers of some of these families in my biweekly Moms' Group, friends and friends of friends with adolescent and adult children adopted from Korea. I know these moms well enough to be convinced that nothing specific they did or failed to do brought on the difficulties they have faced. I also know better than to claim credit for the fact that my family has gotten by without drastic measures. We internationally adoptive families are all in this adventure together, all subject to the same fickle luck.

Among the adoptees who have come through such upheaval, there are plenty of success stories to offer reassurance to families in turmoil. These older and wiser adoptees have not purged themselves of grief, but they have found the vitality needed to reflect on their behavior and the meaning of adoption in their lives. For some of our children, finding that vitality is complicated by other conditions: a long-term clinical depression, hereditary perhaps, that requires ongoing medication; a mental disorder for which the remedies are never totally effective; or an impulsive personality that rubs intimates raw before the rough edge itself is honed down. Those who have to struggle harder are not doomed to lesser lives. Loss and displacement are constant facts of adoptees' lives that will never be erased, but must be integrated into their own deepest awareness of who they are. Although they didn't choose this fate for themselves, they are the only ones who can make personally useful sense of it. That process is ultimately a healthy one.

My resistance to treating adoption as pathology has deep roots that won't budge even with the mighty tugs they get when I read other parents' case study–like accounts of their children's behavior. I have contended most of my life with a rare congenital liver disease, a truly pathological condition that has shaped me in many respects yet doesn't wholly define who I am. I have written a book about chronic illness that I promise not to rewrite here, other than to summarize a lesson that transfers to any life afflicted with suffering. How well people deal with it depends not on the nature or degree of the suffering, but on the strength of their conviction that a life short of perfection is worth living. Parents can help fortify this conviction in so many ways that don't dwell on adoption. Misfortune does not diminish your humanity, but pity and protective hovering make you feel diminished. Parents need to wave aside the smoky plume of adoption issues from time to time and take a good, fresh look at the potential of the human being obscured behind it. Yes, adoption is elemental to our children's lives and their beings, but the meaning *they* make of it as their lives proceed will determine whether it is empowering or victimizing.

3

Holding the Lid on Sorrow and Anger

*I*t's important to me to keep my family's emotions in check. After all, anger only stirs up trouble, and nobody likes a frowning face. I steer clear of sensitive subjects, like my child's birth parents or the fact that he looks different from the rest of us. I prefer to keep life smooth and comfy, to accentuate the positive and leave the negative unsaid. We all get along better that way.

At the opposite extreme from the psychic probers stand the parents who not only refuse to touch but even avert their eyes from anything that might snap back. These are the parents who let sleeping dogs lie, who keep the lid on, who leave well enough alone, who know that some things are better left unsaid, such as the word *adoption* or too much disturbing talk about Tapoda. Families in the habit of glossing over emotionally volatile matters tend to regard their stoicism as a virtue. Adults who give way to "bad" or "negative" feelings are judged weak or self-indulgent. Children who do so are just plain naughty.

If you have been trained to sail through life on an even keel, what do you do with a child who leaps around in the boat? If you let your angry feelings smolder until they die out, how do you raise a child who fans his anger into soaring flames? If happy chit-chat is the best you can offer a dying friend, what do you say to a child who wishes he—or you—were dead? Probably you divert him with happier thoughts, you cajole, you plead, you explain your good intentions. You send him to his room to think about how good he has it, and when he emerges unsubdued, you "lose it" and holler or swear or hit and end up feeling like a failure. Or you preserve the peace and spare yourself by walking away with mouth clamped shut. You leave your child to stew in his own juice, which, given all the heartache it contains, is just too hot and spicy for you.

When I read Jane Jeong Trenka's account in *The Language of Blood* of her strained relationship with her parents, I didn't see them as deliberately cold and mean, but as sadly incapable of bearing intense emotion. When they turned down her request that they attend the memorial service for her birth mother, I read their refusal as self-protective, yes, but not totally dismissive of Jane's right to mourn her mother's death. What would they do if her crying got out of hand? How could they possibly comfort her? What if she blamed it all on them? What if the service made them cry too? How would they ever collect themselves? Best to stay home and not open that can of worms. I have never met her parents, but I believe I recognize them as fellow natives of rural Minnesota, where both the best and the worst of situations are described as "pretty good."

I flashed back on an incident in my own life, the Christmas between my husband's departure and the divorce. To host my family's celebration in the oversized house we had moved into just months before separating, I had to unpack the china that I had packed up so hopefully before the move. As I plucked at the end of the packing tape, I was struck by how drastically my life had changed: I was stuck in a house I couldn't afford, raising two pre-school daughters alone. I didn't want to unpack; I wanted to run away. When I burst into tears, unable to muster the strength to pull back the tape, my mother stepped in to help me. With her head down to avoid my eyes, she muttered, "You'd better get a hold of yourself." I did run away, temporarily, to do just that. I took a walk where I could cry unseen, not only over the stresses of my life, but also over my parents' inability to acknowledge the hurt in it, let alone comfort me. Later, my sister passed on what Mom had said to her: "I just can't stand to see her so sad." My mother was loving in all other respects, and I miss her greatly now that she is gone, but she and I were both shortchanged by a culture that sees intense emotion as a dangerous and demeaning loss of self-control. "Something is rotten in the state of Denmark," as my Danish immigrant grandmother used to comment after some juicy piece of gossip, but what's rotten is the stoicism we "happy Danes" feel obliged to practice.

I told this story to Jane Jeong Trenka and offered her my reading of her parents' seeming coldness. We ended up shaking our heads and laughing over a statistic we have both heard over and over: that Minnesota has the largest number of Korean adoptees per capita of any state in the United States. Thousands of Korean children, by heritage seething cauldrons of *han,* profound and prideful anger at a history of occupation and oppression, have been or are being raised by placid Scandinavian Americans and tight-lipped German Americans, who struggle to keep the lid down and not get scalded. If we take a wider perspective, we see that same mismatch writ large. Imagine the many genetically intense and expressive Tapodans— yelling and sobbing or just talking fast and loud or singing exuberantly, favoring eye-popping colors, craving spicy food—resettled in the relative calm and quiet of Northern cultures: Scandinavia or Germany or the Netherlands or the American Midwest. What cultural contrasts in the realm of emotion distinguish these adopting countries from many of the adoptees' birthplaces!

Of course nature is modified by nurture. Clashes of temperament can settle into a family detente, with the wilder folks somewhat subdued and the duller ones livened up a bit through an even give and take. All families, adoptive or not, have to work to accommodate different temperaments under one roof. Fear of abandonment can skew this effort in adoptive families. Adult adoptees talk about having played the role of perfect child, at least in their elementary school years. If the mention of birth family or country or race troubled their parents, they learned to keep quiet. If displays of sadness or anger hurt their parents or made them mad, they learned to keep their feelings to themselves. Mirim Kim, a Korean American adoptee, has written in an academic thesis about how this role worked in her family and how the problem was finally resolved: "My mother recently told me that her sadness after her father's death made it more difficult to bond with me—an already difficult task considering that I was nearly four years old and had an already-established personality. Not only did her honesty help me to understand her better, but it took away some of the burden I had unconsciously felt in past years—of being the sunshine-child transplanted in order to bring happiness. In acknowledging her own grief, my mother opened up space for me to acknowledge my grief of being a child too young to understand the trauma of losing my culture, language, and family."

In time—usually adolescence or early adulthood—a sunny pretense feels confining and difficult to maintain, yet dropping it is risky. Any sudden burst of genuine feeling may perplex the parents so much that they wonder if their loving child has been kidnapped and replaced by an unruly changeling. Some adoptees who played the role of "sunshine-child" feel unwelcome in their families now unless they hide their true selves behind a smiley mask. The fear of abandonment has become self-fulfilling.

Parents, of course, have their own emotional need to keep family life running smoothly. Once you decide to adopt, you presumably declare an end to the sorrow of childlessness. No matter how firmly you plant your feet on the ground, awaiting your child's arrival is like riding an emotional roller coaster. The ride comes to an exhilarating end when the child whose photo you have fallen in love with appears in the flesh. Your first days, weeks, and months together are as joyous as a honeymoon. Of course you want the ecstasy to last. Glazed over with happiness, you can easily forget that adoption has an obverse side for your child. You marvel at how quickly he has bonded with you and overlook signs of mourning that dawn on you only years later. Even if you're keenly aware of his loss, you gloss it over to protect him from unhappy thoughts. What a surprise, then, when he cries inconsolably or strikes out at you in a fit of temper.

The adoption industry's fondness for euphemisms and upbeat public relations stories reinforces the stoic approach to this deeply emotional experience. Every few years the term that refers to the child's separation from his birth parents is tossed out and replaced with another that better obscures its tragic nature. By the time my children were adopted, terms like *give up, put up for adoption, abandon,* and *relinquish* had been declared taboo. We were advised to tell our children that their birth mothers had *made an adoption plan* for them, even if the "plan" was to leave the child in the bushes at the side of the road. Children feeling the pain of abandonment know instinctively that this carefully crafted phrase is so much romantic mush. They don't ask, "Why did my mother make an adoption plan for me?" but rather, "Why did she give me away?"

If stoicism reigns supreme as your family virtue, you need at least to construct some safety valves for emotion that will keep the family from blowing apart. Declaring certain feelings off limits and certain subjects taboo will just build their implosive momentum. A better choice is to let your child's temperament temper you, to let him help you grow up and learn to express your feelings honestly, and to show you that talk about sensitive but crucial subjects won't incinerate your family.

I entered motherhood determined to comfort my children's every hurt. I wanted to be the loving, nurturing mom they ran to with their sorrows, including the loss of their birth parents and their encounters with racism. But I wasn't ready for anger. No matter how outspoken I can be on paper, face to face I'm nothing but nice. I will go miles out of my way to avoid confrontations. Anger at global injustice emboldens me, but personal discord sets me trembling. So when my children got angry, my first impulse was to quiet them down, to talk sense to them—in other words, to talk them out of their feelings. This is seldom effective, especially with young kids who flail and scream and fall on the floor in public places. My second choice was to scold, to shame them out of their anger. As they got older, I had to learn to let the feelings run and to listen to troubling things I might rather not hear to find out what had aroused such intensity. I came to see that yelling back, when we disagreed, was more honest and effective than talking in falsely calm tones behind clenched teeth. These "fights" cleared the air and ultimately seemed more fair than my efforts at reasoned discipline. They brought out feelings that could have fermented and soured our family life if left unspoken. I'm still not comfortable with anger, but neither am I undone by it.

Between the extremes of hypervigilance and avoidance lies a healthy midpoint where needs are honestly and directly expressed and everyone's emotions are acknowledged. Here too everyone has a right to a decent measure of privacy. Respect for each other as fully emotional human beings serves family relationships better in the long run than control or manipulation. Where "bad" feelings like sorrow and anger are given legitimacy and kept in perspective, "good" feelings can flourish too—feelings like joy and a deeply bonding love.

Cheri Register

4

Parenting on the Defensive

I feel like I'm always on the defensive because my daughter is so full of complaints. She seems to think it's my fault if she's unhappy, and yet I try really hard to stay in control of everything that happens in our family. I explain to her that I mean well, that I have always meant well, and I don't see how I could be wrong. Just think where she'd be if we hadn't adopted her! She should be thankful instead of blaming us all the time.

We well-meaning parents are hardly thrilled to learn that our children are unhappy or disappointed or faring poorly in life. "What did I do wrong?" we ask ourselves as we grope for the quickest fix to the problem. If they persist in being unhappy despite the solutions we offer, we get frustrated and feel inadequate. If they insist on telling us things we'd rather not hear, we feel blamed, maybe even blame*worthy*. Avoiding blame is a human instinct so powerful it may close our ears to what our children are actually telling us. "It's not my fault," we proclaim, maybe implying that our children have made *themselves* unhappy.

Underneath this defensiveness lies a grandiose fallacy about parenthood: the belief that how our children fare in life is a direct measure of our competence. Adoptive parents are especially prone to the myth of the all-powerful parent. When you take on responsibility for a child who wasn't born to you and to whom you had no previous obligation, you become a very deliberate parent, one who has presumably put much forethought into child raising. When you adopt internationally, you agree to an extra set of challenges, such as loving a child of another race whom others in your community, even your family, might think unlovable. It's natural to take pride in being open-minded and generous and willing to charge in where others fear to tread. While some parents decline the moral kudos, others feel entitled to virtue's reward: a happy, loyal, and grateful child.

To be cleared for adoption, you must survive the scrutiny of social workers—that is, if you adopt through an agency concerned with child welfare rather than deal with entrepreneurs in it for the money. You describe how you would handle situation A and prevent situation B until you convince everyone—even yourself—that you can pull off this daunting job. Ideally, your agency equips you to address the tough matters, like race and the existence of birth parents back in Tapoda. Government officials in Tapoda and your own country give you their stamp of approval. You're all set to be a successful parent.

It's easy to see how you might come through this process believing that everything that happens after placement depends solely on you. Whether you've been advised to downplay your child's origins or to emphasize them, you expect that certain actions will have certain predictable consequences. You are in control now. If you stick to the plan, your children will be happy and ever grateful. If they turn out ornery or distant or depressed, well . . . you rack your memory for what you might have done wrong. If you recall some instance where you slipped up, you feel guilty, an unpleasant feeling to bear. If you don't find any wrongdoing, maybe you conclude that your child is the deficient one. In either case, you feel obliged to defend yourself. You meant well. You followed all the expert advice. You did your best. You were a loving parent. How can it be your fault? You're so caught up in absolving yourself that you can't even hear correctly. *Your child isn't blaming you for anything. She's only trying to tell you how she feels.*

Imagine that you're on a family trip to a distant tourist locale. You've looked forward to this trip all through the spring; you've taken time off work and saved up precious family funds to spend. And now, as you travel the long route through an unfamiliar but scenic landscape, your child turns surly on you. You stop for lunch, sure that getting some food in her will lift her mood, but she grumbles even more. You ask her what's wrong, and she whines, "I want to go home. I never wanted to go on this

Cheri Register

trip in the first place." Maybe you launch into a lecture about all the trouble you've gone to, how lucky she is to see sights that other kids never get to see, to have parents who care enough to do fun things with her, things she apparently doesn't even appreciate. If she has enough insight and courage, she might tell you what's really bothering her: That she feels out of place. That she was the only person of color in the café, and people were staring at her. That all the historical sites you've visited are about a history that doesn't include her and the background she comes from. That she hasn't seen one other Tapodan on the whole trip. What do you say to that?

If the guilt is oozing out of you, you want absolution. You can acknowledge it, quickly fend it off, or dispute the cause. Suppose you acknowledge it. "I'm sorry," you protest. "I should have thought of that. How could I not have noticed? Why didn't I think about that ahead of time and choose a different destination? I'm so sorry I hurt you. Mea culpa. Mea culpa. Now please be nice and don't keep punishing me for my mistake with that sour face." The spotlight swings to you and your guilt and shines so steadily on you that she and her feelings become invisible. Your child gets a message you may or may not intend to send: that her discomfort matters less than the huge burden you bear as her ultraresponsible parent.

Maybe you handle guilt by fending it off. "It's not my fault," you argue. "I didn't know who'd be in that café. I can't help it if no Tapodans live around here. I didn't design the history museums. What am I supposed to do about it? It's too bad, but it's just the way things are. You're going to have to get used to it or end up miserable your whole life. Can't we even have a pleasant family vacation without being reminded over and over again how different you feel?"

Maybe you're chagrined that you've let her surliness get to you, and so you make light of it. "Naw," you chuckle, "nobody was looking at you. You're imagining things. If you did see somebody staring, they were probably gawking at that awful lime-green sweater your dad refuses to throw out. Or maybe they think you're beautiful. Take it as a compliment. And history is history. You're here now. That's all that matters. Now cheer up and enjoy yourself. If you can't find some pleasure in this beautiful place, that's *your* problem."

As a recovering perfectionist, I tend toward the first reaction. I have ached over my mistakes and heaped apologies on people I believe I've offended so that they could forgive me and relieve me of the ache. If I was too embarrassed to apologize, I just skulked away and licked my wounds. When my daughters told me they felt uneasy in some situation I had put them in, I felt responsible—and guilty—for my lack of foresight. With experience, though, I've learned a different way to respond: to set aside all thoughts of blame and guilt and simply *listen.* I can now imagine a different outcome to the scenario: "You know, you're right. We *have* been traveling through some pretty isolated and provincial places. At least the scenery is spectacular and we've had some good family moments. But let's think about spending our next vacation somewhere more enjoyable for you."

Listening with ears open and mouth shut, without apologies or advice or quick fixes, is hard to do. Hearing the sorrow or the anger or the pain and just letting it be can leave you feeling powerless. Aren't we parents *supposed* to have the answers? Mirim Kim, an adoptee, experienced our predicament while she was working as a camp counselor with teenage Korean adoptees, one of whom became sad and inconsolable: "Now the comforter, I catch a glimpse of the anguish parents must feel watching their precious beloved child suffer—and the inadequacy in not being able to take away the pain. But I've been there, I've been where she's at now, and I was only told to 'give it to God' or to not let it bother me. To not 'let them win.' And what I wanted at that time, most desperately of all, was simply to be understood."

Unless we were adopted ourselves, there's much about our children's lives we *don't* understand and can barely imagine. Our mothers didn't disappear into the crowd after giving birth to us. We were never separated from our siblings and left in a strange place with the puzzling promise of a new home and family. Most of us were raised by parents who resembled us, not only in race but in facial features and body type. Few of us have been purred over as strange, rare specimens or scorned as unwelcome foreigners. We enjoy the privileges of life in the mainstream. We can hardly claim to *know* what our children are going through, let alone control it. Our best source of information is their testimony.

Of course, that testimony isn't always entirely reliable. Our children may well heap blame on us and hold us accountable for sorrows over which we have no control. Sometimes they do this to manipulate us: "If you were my real parents, you would love me enough to buy me that." Sometimes casting blame on us relieves them of feelings they can't bear. Whether we're guilty or not is irrelevant, and arguing the case only gets us more deeply mired. Instead, we need to learn how to hear the charges without internalizing them and disliking ourselves or the child. One mother I know felt like a punching bag all through her daughter's adolescence. She acquired that role, I believe, because she was the most securely grounded and resilient person in her daughter's life. After the daughter grew up and left home and found a career that made her feel competent and purposeful, she returned with a gift for her mother. "Thank you for putting up with me," she said. "I just felt so angry, and I didn't know it wasn't your fault." We would be foolish to insist on gratitude, but wise to treasure it when it comes our way.

It has become easier for me to listen as my daughters have grown more articulate and reflective, less inclined to tangle their words in shouts and whines that feel like accusations. Still, I get twinges of "What should I have done?" or "Why didn't I think of that?" I've found it helpful to broaden the context, to take the focus off our particular family and look at the larger dynamics. Listening to what other adoptees have to say has been tremendously helpful.

In the summer of 2002 I was invited to speak at the annual conference of KAAN (Korean American Adoptee Adoptive Family Network), a U.S. coalition founded in 1998. I hadn't attended an adoption conference in several years, and I noticed immediately how the makeup of the audience had changed. About a quarter of the people at my workshop were adult adoptees. I was delighted to see them there and impressed by the bold, articulate voices I heard throughout the conference. Their testimony ranged from the raw, intense candor of young adults newly aware of the injustices in their lives to the seasoned wisdom of those who had spent time examining how international adoption had shaped them. I had read newspaper and magazine articles by adult adoptees and memoir pieces and poetry in recently published anthologies, so I was not surprised to hear critiques of some of the old truths that govern adoptive parenting, together with calls for an end to international adoption from Korea, a modern, increasingly wealthy country that should be able to provide for all its children.

I *was* surprised, however, by the defensive responses of many of the parents at the conference. Some spoke as if they were being called to account personally for any troubles the adoptees reported. A few adoptees-only sessions had been set up to allow them to speak their minds and hearts without getting sidetracked into parental concerns. This practice was familiar to me from my younger days as a social activist. I remember when Black people in the civil rights movement chose to meet separately, without white liberal voices, and when women organized consciousness-raising groups free of men's influence. The historian Sara Evans of the University of Minnesota, an adoptive mother herself, has traced this use of "free social space" far back in U.S. history, where it has been essential to the exercise of democracy. Yet many parents at the KAAN conference took umbrage at being excluded. Parents of young children wanted to listen in and ask questions so they could learn how to do right by their own kids. Some parents of adult children fretted about what might be said in these secret chambers, where they would have no chance to defend themselves. Curiously, the adoptee panels that *were* open to parents drew few of them. "I don't want to hear what a terrible person I am," one mother blurted at the closing evaluation session. Others agreed that they certainly didn't enjoy being blamed for everything.

The tension in the air and the suspicion of adoptees' motives gave me pause. What are these parents afraid of, I wondered, and why would they begrudge our collective children the right to speak freely with each other? Did they allow their kids privacy at home, or did they eavesdrop at their bedroom doors when they had friends over and pry in their diaries when they were away? Did they encourage their kids to trust their experience and speak their minds, or did they shush them up when they disagreed? Did they fear their family bonds would break without constant togetherness? And why did they think that when adoptees get together, all they do is bash their parents? They have so much else to talk about.

And so do we. We parents ought to be talking among ourselves about how *we* will endure over the long haul as

Cheri Register

our children grow up and away and venture into worlds unfamiliar to us. If we're honest about our fears, we can take comfort in knowing they are shared. Jane Lazarre, a white woman married to an African American man and the mother by birth of two adult sons, has written a book, *Beyond the Whiteness of Whiteness,* in which she talks candidly about the distance that race creates between herself and her children. When her son told her that she can't possibly understand him because she's white, she felt "exiled" from her family. "Fierce possessiveness lies at the heart of motherhood," she writes, "right alongside the more reasonable need to see one's children become themselves, and now this emotion rises up and chokes me, obliterating vocabulary. I cannot find words to express my feelings, or my feelings are too threatening to find easy language. They are minefields lining opposite sides of the road of my motherhood of this beloved son. What is this whiteness that threatens to separate me from my own child?" Lazarre thinks of her whiteness as "a sun-blinded desert of distance" between herself and her children. We white parents with children of color are "sun-blinded" not only by our race, but also by our preconceptions of what it means to be adopted, an experience few of us know firsthand. We will never know our children's hearts and minds through and through, but neither do we need to control them to love them. Liberation from the myth of omnipotence is a good deed we parents can perform for each other.

Jane Lazarre calls for "the patience to listen to the multitude of details making up stories not your own. It is not that we cannot understand each other, but that we presume that understanding too quickly, close the unfamiliar story down with our own intrusive narrating." If we listen patiently to adult adoptees, we will hear a clearer, deeper message no longer obscured by the static of guilt and defensiveness. We might even hear something new and valuable that provokes us to reexamine our own experience. In an open letter to a friend who committed suicide published in the anthology *Seeds from a Silent Tree,* Kari Ruth, a Korean American adoptee, writes, "Those parents must not understand that the price they paid for us was insignificant compared to the price we pay to fit into their world." In that one line, she turns the relation between parent and child on its head. We expect our children to be grateful to us for plucking them out of isolation and poverty in Tapoda and raising them as our own, but how often do we thank them for allowing us the family we longed for?

As we listen without defensiveness to our adult children, and as we talk honestly with each other, we run up against larger questions about this social experiment we are all living through. Kari Ruth's comment reminds us that international adoption is not simply a matter of child welfare, but also a means of supplying would-be parents with children. This ambiguity puts some parents on the defensive. They don't like to hear criticism of international adoption, especially from its beneficiaries. One of the foremost critics is Tobias Hübinette, a Korean Swedish adoptee with sound academic credentials who analyzes adoption as a form of colonialism in which the human resources of the poorer countries fill the needs of the richer countries. Some of the parents who hear him speak at conferences or read his posts on the Internet demean the messenger rather than listen to the message. They judge him too angry or too radical, or they give him a condescending pat on the back as they speculate about his upbringing. His discontent with international adoption, they decide, must be his parents' fault.

Of course it's hard to hear that your actions have helped perpetrate an injustice, even without your intent. You feel blamed, labeled unethical, immoral, a fundamentally bad person. But this is not about you; it's about the injustice. You are blameworthy only if you refuse to listen. Human beings live with moral ambiguity all the time, even in Tapoda. Few of us leave our home countries when our governments engage in policies that trouble us. We adhere to religious faiths that others cite to justify abhorrent behavior. We tolerate scoundrels in our family circle. Ambiguity is a fact of life. That's not your fault.

5

Believing Race Doesn't Matter

Life would be a lot more peaceful if we were all color-blind, so I don't pay much attention to race. I rarely think of my son as Tapodan; he's just my son. If he comes home and tells me that somebody at school called him a racist name, I tell him it doesn't mean a thing. That person just feels insecure about himself. He could as easily have picked on somebody with a bad haircut or big feet. Everybody gets teased about something. Kids can be ruthless, but we all survive. It's best just to let it go.

Within months of your child's arrival, a wonderful transformation takes place. You are swinging him in the park
one day when a stranger approaches and asks, "Where's
he from?" The question takes you aback. How can she
tell he's adopted? you puzzle, and then you chuckle to
yourself. You have forgotten that he looks Tapodan.
When you peer into his face now or catch a glimpse of
him across the room, you don't see a child of another
race. You see your own little Stevie or Staffan or Etienne.
Race doesn't figure into your perception at all. Before
you adopted—and this is something you don't like to
admit—when a person of another race entered your
line of vision, certain words popped into your head to
announce the fact: color names, geographical words,
maybe even old racial slurs you would never say aloud.
Your shoulders tensed a little. Maybe you smiled a bit
too broadly as you cleared away the first signals, like skin
color and hair texture, to see the individual at hand. But
now, familiarity with your own sweet child has altered
your vision. You have integrated a Tapodan into your
family so thoroughly that race no longer matters. Loving
transracially has made you color-blind.

Cheri Register

Please don't get too comfortable with this illusion, because it's dangerous for your child, who is undergoing a transformation of his own. He is developing a self-image by watching you, his family, the people with whom he's most intimate. When he is old enough to envision himself as a being separate from you, he may nevertheless imagine himself in your skin. A peek in the mirror or a glimpse of himself in a family photo can come as a shock. He doesn't see Stevie or Staffan or Etienne, but a strange boy with features different from what he has imagined. The result is the identity confusion that transracial adoptees from Asia call "banana" or "Twinkie" and those of African origin call "Oreo." Inside and outside don't match up.

The sociologist David Woodger—born in Gujarat, India, adopted in England, and a founder of the Association of Transracially Adopted Persons (ATRAP)—offered the audience at a 2003 conference on "The Meaning of Roots" in Copenhagen a telling illustration of how this confusion plays out. A friend of his, also an Indian adoptee (regarded as "black" in the United Kingdom), noticed one day that his habit on entering a bus or a subway was to look for a seat next to a white person, someone who looked cozy and familiar, like his family. Yet when he was alone in a seat, the people most likely to sit down next to him were black. No matter what self-image an international adoptee carries out into the world, a racial identity will be thrust upon him by others' perceptions.

Color-blind or not, we still have to respond to that first big public encounter, the first time our child is called a racist name or teased about his appearance. Our best instincts are to protect and reassure. Say your child comes home from school and tells you that a playground bully called him a dirty Podog. Your first concern is to ease his shame and fear. You certainly don't want to tell him that you too learned the term *dirty Podog* in elementary school but never thought then about the harm it might do, since there were no Tapodans around. Now that you're raising one, you want to defuse the term of its power to hurt. What the bully said doesn't matter, you say. He just felt like picking on somebody, and he grabbed at one thing your son has that he doesn't. He could just as easily have picked on a girl with glasses or a boy shorter than himself. In fact, *you* used to get bullied for your strawlike hair.

These bullies act tough, but inside they're suffering from low self-esteem. The only way they can feel important is by putting other kids down. Maybe he's jealous of your son's Tapodan good looks.

Weeks go by and you learn that the bullying hasn't stopped. Your son doesn't tell you, but one of his friends drops the hint. Several kids are involved, and they've composed a little chant about Tapodans. The water-off-a-duck's-back approach isn't doing its job, so you opt for intervention. This is a problem for the school to take on. Someone has to teach these kids that there is nothing wrong with looking different and that Tapodans are the same as everyone else under the skin. You offer yourself as the teacher, and you bring your collection of Tapodan artifacts to school and read the class a book about Tapoda. With a bit of struggle and cajoling, you even get your son into his traditional Tapodan outfit. And that's the end of it. He has no more complaints about being bullied.

Or so you think. In a broad study of American internationally adoptive families under way at the University of Minnesota, the psychologist Richard Lee, one of the co-investigators, has found that while most of the parents surveyed described themselves as "racially aware," only 20 percent reported that their children had encountered racial comments. He suspects a discrepancy here, since the reality is likely closer to 100 percent. I have a hunch about this discrepancy. Only a few years ago, my daughter admitted that she had been bullied with racial epithets in elementary school by one large older girl. She kept quiet about it at home for fear that I would come to school and make a scene and get her in even deeper trouble. Instead, she tried to steer clear of the bully and kept herself surrounded by friends at recess. Though she came to me readily with other problems, she guessed that I wouldn't have the right answer for this one because it could never happen to me.

She was right. I *would* have overreacted, never having learned that the dailiness of race requires you to pick which battles are worth fighting and to devise strategies that will get you through the minefield safely. Rich Lee has observed that internationally adoptive parents feel more confident educating their children about their ethnicity than talking to them about racism. Although I have fancied myself enlightened about race, my daughters have taught me never to underestimate my ignorance about the type and extent of the racism they face and the pervasive sense of otherness they live with as Asians in a predominantly European environment. In the classic essay "Notes of a Native Son," part of a book by the same title, James Baldwin offered the boldest, most heart-rending statement I have ever read of the obligation that parents of African American children bear: "how to prepare the child for the day when the child would be despised and how to *create* in the child—by what means?—a stronger antidote to this poison than one had found for oneself." Prepare our children to be despised? Can we white parents fathom such a task?

David Woodger urges parents to consider the shocking distance between the inclusive comfort of our families and the harsh, exclusive environment outside. Parents of color train their children to negotiate this distance, but we white parents haven't had to acquire those skills ourselves. We believe that raising our children to feel loved and comfortable and secure at home will equip them to feel strong and confident elsewhere. The Korean Norwegian Geir Follevåg, in his book *Adoptert Identitet,* faults his childhood as too idyllic. He was told that he was simply Norwegian, that he should ignore all teasing focused on his appearance and feel sorry for the people who teased him. "I was tricked," he writes, "and I tricked myself into believing that my foreign appearance was not important to take a stand on. . . . I avoided confronting what it meant to be in a situation such as I was in." When he left the protection of home to attend high school in a larger town, the racist taunting he encountered there nearly destroyed him. Yet he sees those three years as the most constructive in his life because he had to come to terms with his Asian appearance and rid himself of the racism he had internalized by thinking it unimportant.

Color blindness is a luxury our children can't afford. Although they have been raised in our families with whatever privileges we white parents claim for ourselves—material riches, well-maintained neighborhoods, good schools—away from home they take on the color of whichever ethnic or immigrant group they most resemble. On the bus your Tapodan son, in his casual pants and athletic shirt, is just another refugee to be pitied for his tragic rootlessness or reviled for supposedly taking jobs and government resources from hard-working native citizens. Alone on the street in a white neighborhood or driving a car in the dark of night, he becomes someone to fear and watch with suspicion. James Baldwin's essay also describes what it was like to learn that his very being struck fear in other people and to realize how dangerous this was for himself. "Notes of a Native Son" should be required reading for prospective parents adopting transracially.

Baldwin's essay was written in 1955, on the verge of the civil rights movement in the United States. We can persuade ourselves that conditions have improved, that racism is no longer so virulent as it was then. Our children know, however, that danger is always close at hand. What do we make of the pick-up lines from men who assume all Asian women are sexually submissive just because some have had to turn to prostitution to endure poverty and the devastation of war? In European countries where sex tourism is freely advertised and where Asian women have been brought to work as prostitutes, the lines are more blatantly offensive. Charlotte Gullach, a Korean Danish adoptee whom I heard speak at a conference in Copenhagen, has "heard everything from 'What

do you cost?' to 'I have never tried your kind before.'"
Anti-immigrant and ethnic-purity movements threaten
international adoptees as well. A neo-Nazi political party
in Norway has called for the sterilization of adoptees who
refuse to return to their birth countries.

My daughters have taught me that racial epithets and
overt bullying are no more hurtful than the supposedly
benign reminders that they don't really belong here: The
eager queries like "Where are you from?" The kindly com-
pliments on their mastery of English. The expectation that
they will want to hear all about your trip to Japan or your
lovely Vietnamese daughter-in-law. The gushing intro-
ductions that conclude, "She's adopted from Korea."

As our children near adulthood, many of them are
attracted to immigrant and ethnic communities where
they can blend in with a crowd for once. This troubles
some parents, who worry that their children will settle in
a place where they themselves aren't welcome or at least
aren't comfortable. Roles are reversed, and the parents get
an inkling of what it is like to be the *other, different, ethnic,* an *outsider,* a *minority.* Parents who raised their children color-blind—or, more truthfully, as honorary white

people of their own ethnic persuasion—may be dismayed to watch them grow into adult Tapodans, as though their failure to turn white, or at least behave like "us," is a form of rejection.

Moving into these communities is no easy matter for our children, however, who risk being rejected by their "own" people. Some seek out way stations where the risk is minimized. They find acceptance in multicultural settings where being a person of color or of foreign heritage takes primacy over being Tapodan. Latino groups in academe or the arts, for example, unite people of various national origins. Some adoptees feel safer venturing into pan-Asian or Asian and Pacific Islander organizations than those limited to people of their specific ethnicity. Many Korean adoptees from exclusively white areas of the United States migrate to the West Coast, not only to Los Angeles's Koreatown, but also to San Francisco's predominantly Chinese neighborhoods, where they can experience the sensation of blending into the crowd without having to explain their lack of Korean language and social manners. Adoptees who have returned to Korea enjoy vacationing in other Asian countries, where they can relax among black-haired and golden-skinned people who assume they are "Korean Koreans," as my daughter calls them, or *kyopos* living in the countries whose passports they carry.

We should be thankful for any welcome our children receive from fellow Tapodans-in-exile or from people of their race who have spent generations claiming and defending their entitlement to full citizenship in *this* country. They have no obligation to our children, but they do have much to teach them. The college course that probably did the most to round my daughter into a confident, self-sufficient, educated adult was Asian American history. It gave her a context in which to place her experience and make clearer sense of it. She learned that Asians in America are treated as "perpetual foreigners" and could offer her own examples of how that works. As she read aloud from her assignments on the Chinese Exclusion Acts and the internment of Japanese Americans in World War II, I wondered why, in all the programs designed to make her proud of her Korean heritage—the summer culture camp, the post-adoption groups, the family homeland tour—no one had ever suggested resources

Cheri Register

to help her fit into a more accurate and suitable identity, Asian American.

I learned a few things from that class too. One day I casually referred to a story in the newspaper about a pair of Siamese twins. "The word is *conjoined*, Mom," my daughter corrected me quietly. This gave me pause to think about Chang and Eng and their lives as circus freaks and why this rare phenomenon should be forever identified as a bizarre ethnic peculiarity. Even though the Dionne sisters were raised in a sort of theme park, where tourists could come at designated hours and watch them play, we don't call quintuplets "Canadians."

We white folks claim a right of definition that reserves normality to us. All human groups do the same, but where one group's view dominates, the result is racism, even within transracially adoptive families. Our children are "different" from us, we think. We seldom regard ourselves as "different" from them. They are "nonwhite," but we do not call ourselves "non-Tapodan." They are "minorities," even though, on an international scale, people who look like them might outnumber people who look like us. They are "people of color," which means that we are "people of no color." In calling ourselves "white," despite our pink or beige or olive hues, we imagine ourselves unmarked by race, humanity distilled to its purest, most natural form. Everyone else is named and defined according to how they deviate from the basic human type we presume to be. We are indeed color-blind, but it's our own color we're blind to. In fact, we are racially marked in the extreme. How and where we live, how we see the world, what we believe, what we take for granted, what we fear, the way we walk and speak, the values we hold dear—all depend on our whiteness.

Listening to our kids, trying to see the world through their eyes, can help us begin to understand what Jane Lazarre means by "the sun-blinded desert of whiteness." I remember a moment from my daughter's childhood that altered my vision for a while. We were baking cookies— oatmeal scotchies—and she looked into the bowl of batter and announced, "It's skin color." I didn't see the "flesh" of my childhood crayon box, but butterscotch, the color of *her* skin. I took off on a flight of fancy, imagining how the world would look with butterscotch skin as the norm, which, by sheer numbers, it actually is. My skin paled in

Cheri Register

comparison, not to white but to a sallow, splotchy mixture of pink and orange with prominent blue veins running underneath. I thought about the traits that define me, not only how white and European American they are, but how Scandinavian Minnesotan rural working-class—the particular variety of white I am.

A second incident knocked my vision off its habitual pivot point. Mrs. Hyun Sook Han of Children's Home Society of Minnesota was telling stories about her childhood during the Korean War, many of which are retold in her memoir, *Many Lives Intertwined*. One hot day some white soldiers were cooling themselves off at the well, and they had taken off their shirts—something Korean men would never have done in public. "Why are they so hairy?" Hyun Sook asked her grandmother. "Because they're closer to the monkeys than we are," her grandmother replied. It's good to be reminded that not everyone participates in our illusion that we are the pinnacle of humanity.

We may not be able to protect our children from racism. We may not know how to teach them the best strategies for countering racism. We can't convey to them the essence of being Tapodan. But we can and must examine our whiteness and see how it has benefited or limited us as parents and what impact it has on our children. Those parents, for example, who feel rejected when their children seek companionship in communities of their own race or ethnicity apparently believe that anyone invited to mingle with the white people, to become an honorary white person, should be thrilled with the privilege. They take "No, thank you" as an aberrant answer. That too is racism.

Yes, I know that racism isn't exclusive to white people, that people of all races practice it. Yes, I know that people who look alike to us make racial distinctions among themselves. The genocide in Bosnia and Rwanda are proof of that. But the racism our children encounter has a concrete history. It is the heritage of European colonialism, the harvesting of the resources of part of the world to enrich the other part. The colonizers seized, by force, the privilege of dividing humanity into categories, identifying and naming these "races," designating who belonged to which, and describing the traits they considered natural to each of them. When a playground bully pulls out one of those old stereotypes and flings it at your child, he is drawing on that history.

Cheri Register

International adoption itself is a legacy of European colonialism, a function of racism, of white privilege. My daughter was telling me and a friend of hers about a colleague at the coffee shop where she works who had objected to the employee dress code. He refused to tie back his dreadlocks because they're an expression of his spirituality. "Is he a white guy?" her friend asked derisively. Yes, he was. We talked briefly about white people who appropriate bits and pieces of other cultures' religious beliefs. "He just wants to make himself more interesting," her friend conjectured. "Maybe he was adopted by Rastafarians," I heard myself say. I had meant it to sound absurd, but instead the words stopped me. Why is that absurd? Jamaica allows children to be adopted abroad. Why should we laugh at the vision of Rastafarians or any other Jamaicans coming to claim white babies? I thought about the movie *The Jerk* and wondered—Steve Martin's performance aside—why the premise of a white man thinking himself black because he was raised in a black family should be funny. Isn't that our children's life story?

This imbalance should be evidence enough that racism is a matter of political and economic power and not simply a psychological defense mechanism for people of low self-esteem, as the "color-blind" parents portray it to their children We parents frequently ask ourselves how our children's lives have been changed by adoption. We imagine them growing up on the street and dying early deaths of disease or brutality. Or we imagine them struggling to find their place in the pecking order in an overcrowded orphanage, then being turned out as teenagers to make their own livings. Maybe we see them in their birth families, loved and nurtured, but destined always to be poor. We may conduct this exercise to gloat over the good deed we have done or to justify a choice we feel ambivalent about. Or we might use it to keep our children in line: "Where would you be without us?"

There is a better reason to think this through and to undergird the images with factual information about the conditions that lead to adoption and the perils children face both at home and abroad: so that we see what's wrong with this picture and begin to examine the white privilege that allows us to play savior of the world. If you don't see it, your child will one day point it out to you. That gift of sight is one of the greatest rewards an internationally adoptive parent ever receives.

6

Keeping Our Children Exotic

~

I'm so proud of my precious angel, who came all this distance to join our family. What a little doll she is, with her sweet Tapodan smile and her lovely Tapodan skin and hair and sparkly eyes. It's so much fun to dress her up in her traditional Tapodan outfit and watch other people delight in her beauty. What a little ambassador for Tapoda she has become! I always take extra care to remind her how special she is.

Many of us parents, advised to "celebrate the difference," nod in quick agreement. This attitude seems more honest and realistic than color blindness. Yet with our limited knowledge of what celebrating the difference entails, we easily stray down a path that dead-ends in exotic isolation. We interpret "difference" to be special or unique and connect "celebrate" with celebrations and festivals. And so we dress up our children in Tapodan costumes, coach them in Tapodan songs and dances, and buy them books of Tapodan folktales. Seldom ranging far from home, we still manage to purvey a bit of Tapodan culture to our families. We have at our service a cottage industry of Tapodan artifacts designed for the adoption market. We find resources on the Internet, including discussion groups where we can exchange ideas with other non-Tapodan parents about how to incorporate Tapodan culture into our family life: how to celebrate holidays, how to play Tapodan games, how to cook Tapodan delicacies.

This enthusiasm is a suitable beginning for young children, but if we stop there, we have merely adorned them in Western perceptions of Tapodan heritage—an archaic and stereotypical "museum culture"—without tapping into the actual, living, evolving, contemporary Tapoda. If discomfort with the unfamiliar prevents us from making extended visits to Tapoda or genuine connections with ethnic communities, the little mock Tapoda we create at home, or among other adoptive families, has to suffice as our children's ethnic identity. But it's a fantasy Tapoda, a selective assortment of features that suit our values, with the harsh and distasteful and troublesome cautiously omitted.

The child who emerges from this effort is a bit like Frankenstein's monster, wired together from the trappings of Tapodan material culture that we foreigners most easily grasp, but with no Tapodan heart or soul, nothing of the value system, beliefs, interpersonal behavior, or outlook on life that undergirds day-to-day life in Tapoda. Of course, this child is far more appealing than Frankenstein's monster. She is beautiful in her Tapodan dress, so talented at Tapodan song and dance, so cute when she pronounces "hello" and "thank you," the only Tapodan words she knows. Everyone who meets her eagerly embraces her. They celebrate her difference because it doesn't challenge their place in the mainstream.

And they convince themselves that accepting her, the cute little alien in their midst, makes them better, more tolerant, more generous human beings. If she's the only one of her kind in her high school, she stands a good chance of being elected Homecoming Queen.

There are tough words for this phenomenon: *tokenism, fetishism, exoticism, infantilization.* Asian adoptees call it *Orientalism* or *China doll syndrome,* a whitewashed substitute for being truly Chinese or any other variety of Asian. "China doll" is an impractical identity that requires docility, charm, unfailing courtesy, and other traits that adhere to the stereotype, including one that burdens girls as they enter adolescence: a sexually seductive innocence. On the rounds to promote her book, *The Language of Blood,* Jane Jeong Trenka heard female adoptees tell about being mistaken for their middle-aged fathers' trophy wives. A casual arm around the shoulder or peck on the cheek can have embarrassing consequences. Asian men, by contrast, are regarded as childlike and sexless. The anthropologist Rae Eikelboom, a Korean Dutch adoptee, has found in his research that Asian men "are perceived as beautiful in terms of elegant, smoothly coloured, harmonious, etc., but not in erotic terms. Here in Europe Asian men are not seen and portrayed (for example in movies) as sexual beings who are sexy to (western) women. The movies in which Asian men perform the role of the sexy masculine hero, instead of a rather ridiculous kung fu guy who makes weird sounds when he flies through the air, are countable on one hand." When Korean Norwegian Geir Follevåg grew his hair long and tied it at the nape of his neck, people began trying out their Spanish on him. Latin lover, unfortunately, is no less confining a stereotype.

The sweet little angel from afar is also an *isolating* identity. A fake Tapodan molded out of foreign perceptions of her heritage will not fit in comfortably among other Tapodans. And the expectation that she always be the cute little Tapodan in our midst denies her full entitlement to her adoptive culture. There will come a time when she demands to be just herself, free of ethnic adornment, just a teenager, most likely, who is Canadian or Dutch or Australian or French first of all, like her peers. If it doesn't happen in the teenage years, adulthood will put an end to being perpetually little and cute.

Yet her parents may have a stake in maintaining the façade. Maybe selecting certain aspects of her ethnicity to celebrate eases their discomfort with the fact that she doesn't resemble them. Maybe she's the only adopted child in a family of birth siblings, and emphasizing her specialness is how the family makes a place for her. Maybe she's the long-awaited girl in a family of boys, and the Tapodan femininity her parents ascribe to her suits their dream. Maybe she has become their goodwill ambassador and opened doors in their community that will slam shut if she turns into an ordinary local kid. Maybe creating a Tapodan heritage is an important family pastime that depends on her unwhining compliance. When Mom manages the dance group's rehearsal and performance schedule, her daughter's refusal to dance is a huge embarrassment.

The risk of distorting our children's ethnic identity doesn't free us of our obligation to form a genuine appreciation of their Tapodan heritage. Among the sorrows that many adult adoptees bear is ignorance of their cultural origins, of how people live and behave in their birth countries, of ethnic underpinnings that help answer the question, "Who am I?" No one, I believe, should be allowed to adopt internationally without an expressed willingness to learn what it means to be Tapodan and to allow their children access to the culture of their birth. But we must not overestimate our ability to deliver a culture we have never lived. Our perceptions and judgments of Tapodan culture are culturally determined. One telling example of this is parents' eagerness to buy artifacts that represent our children's birth cultures. We learn, we act, we declare what's important to us by buying things. The stuff we buy says as much about Western consumerism as it does about Tapoda.

Yet buy we must. If we live at a distance from the culture itself, objects may have to stand in for firsthand experience. My house, too, is decorated with Korean wall hangings and stocked with Korean folktales in translation and soy sauce and sesame oil. They are convenient reminders of that other place that is a crucial piece of our family's history. Our hallway closet offers a choice of *hanbok,* from the shiny, gaudy toddler size up to the understated, elegant blue one that one daughter wears when an occasion arises. For the other daughter, a simple amethyst pendant mined, made, and bought in Korea is ethnic fashion statement enough.

Culture camps organized by and for adoptive families help instill a sense of heritage, not least because they allow our "special" children, gathered en masse, to be "normal" for a week out of the year. The hot brilliance of the spotlight dissipates into a warm, illuminating glow. My daughters attended Korean culture camp every summer through elementary school and continued on for a few years as teen helpers. They're glad they did. So am I, and I relished the days I spent there as a volunteer. Until we took a trip to Korea when they were teenagers, culture camp was our most direct experience of things Korean. Every year my daughters learned, and then forgot again, the name of the national hero who commanded the Turtle Ship in that war with Japan or China back in whatever century that was. The lessons in folding paper cranes and balloons took firmer hold, though they were lost on me. But culture camp didn't teach them how Korea is governed today or that Korean people are more likely to make their living in manufacturing or business or high-tech communications than in rice farming. The images of ancient and rural Korea implanted in their minds didn't prepare them for the massive apartment complexes, heavy traffic, and ubiquitous cell phone use they saw in Seoul on our family trip. La Semana, a Latin American culture camp I visited years ago, seemed to do better at portraying the contemporary culture of the countries involved.

It's time for adult adoptees, if they're willing, to assume the management of the camps and design a curriculum that prepares children for real life. The older adoptees have tested out the "celebrated differences" that served as their ethnic identity. Mark Hagland, a Korean American adoptee who writes for *Korean Quarterly,* long thought of himself as a "fake Korean" and put off visiting Korea for fear he'd be treated "badly." The time he spent there left him with "a bemused half-foreignness" and the realization that he will always live with "a split-screen identity." *How* to live on a split screen sounds like a valid lesson for culture camp.

Though some of the curriculum at our culture camp was borrowed from the Saturday schools established by Korean American immigrants, our camp rarely drew children from immigrant families, who live out the most deeply seated aspects of Korean culture every day. Forming relationships with an ethnic community is far more difficult than falling back on the museum culture of our own making. I would probably get a D in this aspect of adoptive parenting, unless eating with gusto at Korean restaurants earns extra credit. I'm just too shy for the job. I make friends passively, after discovering common interests over time with people I happen to meet. I've never had the gumption to chat up Korean American strangers and invite them to be role models for my children. It's not only a question of shyness. Holding back a bit is more diplomatic. I cringe when I see adoptive parents charge into immigrant communities as though they expect an instant welcome and even congratulations and gratitude for what they have done. The Tapodans themselves may regard the adoption of their country's children as cause for sorrow or shame or animosity.

Fortunately, a few parents with outgoing personalities and intercultural sensitivity have established connections for the rest of us. Over the years, some steady bridge-building between adoptive families and ethnic communities has made it easier for our children to pass from one to the other. Friends of Korea, a service organization in Sacramento, California, tries to establish *reciprocal* relationships. Its founder, Chris Winston, explains, "Instead of behaving like an adoption support group, being fed information by those in-the-know about Korean heritage and culture, we . . . tried for a different model, a mutual support society where we attempted to determine Korean community needs and fit those needs into the fabric of our programs." For instance, adoptive parent volunteers have coached elderly Korean Americans preparing for their U.S. citizenship exams.

The good example closest to home from which my family has reaped the most benefit is the newspaper *Korean Quarterly.* Out of deeply felt motivation, stunning persistence, and skillful diplomacy, two adoptive parents—Martha Vickery, a writer and editor, and her husband, the photographer Stephen Wunrow—created a newspaper based in Minnesota but with an international readership of adoptive families, adult adoptees, Korean Americans, and Korean nationals. *Korean Quarterly* is a forum for adult adoptees and the children of immigrants to talk honestly about feeling marginal in both countries and for Koreans to write both affectionately and critically about their culture. It also keeps its readers up-to-date and invested in political and economic issues in South and North Korea. Its advertisements attest to the growth of a Korean American community broad enough to include adoptive families. Yet Vickery is cautious about claiming success. Readers of the newspaper, she says, constitute a "virtual community" that might cease to exist if it stopped publishing.

There is no better cultural education than travel—not the pampered tourism that whisks you from the Sheraton to the Sofitel, but a trip that brings you into as close contact as possible with Tapodan daily life. A trip to the birth country not only allows your child an unfiltered view of its culture, but begins to fill a void in her personal history by exposing the circumstances that lead to international adoption. Up close, she gets to see both Tapoda's radiant beauty and its murky shadows. The country is both more complex and more interesting than the glossy, pick-and-choose version you have constructed at home. Reality will serve your child far better in the long run than an ill-fitting pretense. International travel is, of course, expensive, and added on to the costs of the adoption itself, it might seem like more than your family finances can bear. This problem ought to be addressed before adopting: How much belt-tightening will you do to afford this trip that is so vital to your child?

A question that comes up again and again in adoptive parent chat rooms and on e-mail lists is: How hard should I push my child to take an interest in her birth culture if she doesn't want to? I would not push a child to perform as the exotic little angel from afar, no matter how entertaining friends and family find these displays. I would not push her to wear her Tapodan dress if she's more comfortable in jeans, like the other kids. I would not push her to sing in the Tapodan chorus if she would rather run up and down a soccer field. I would not push her to choose Tapoda as the subject of her school report if she is fascinated with some other country. I may, indeed, have done these things, but I wouldn't do them again.

At the same time, I *would* expect my child to take part in activities that are of deep and abiding importance to our family. By mid elementary school children can sense when their parents are genuinely interested and when they are putting on a show. In *A Single Square Picture* Katy Robinson writes that the first time her parents took her to an annual Asian festival, she was happy to be there. By the third year, she refused to go because it made her "feel stupid": "There were no other Asians in my neighborhood. My parents didn't have any Asian friends. I figure my parents didn't like them much either. . . . My dad tried too hard, his loud chuckle strained as he said, 'Katy, this man is from Korea, just like you!'" Ask yourself, would you still go see that Bollywood movie even if your child adopted from India refused to go along? Do you intend to read Anchee Min's new book yourself even if your Chinese-born daughter never lifts the cover? Do you enjoy listening to those Andean panpipes even after your Peruvian-born child has retreated to the bedroom and flipped on the Top 40 station? Your independent interest in these features of your child's birth culture will demonstrate to her that they are inherently valuable, not just foreign idiosyncrasies that she is obligated by birth to revere. By the same token, if you can't stomach durian or bitter melon, you can respectfully decline to eat it without disparaging the entire cuisine. Your child may even take pride in being more venturesome than her parents. Even if our children shy away from all reminders of their birth culture during the years when their peers' tastes are all-important, they will be glad, in the long run, that we hung on, that we truly cared about the country of their birth because we love them and everything that makes them who they are.

By virtue of being displaced from one country to another or being people of color or of pronounced ethnic features in white families, our children have mixed or multiple identities. During childhood and adolescence and into young adulthood, they will discard some and try on others, then pick up one of the discards and shake it out to make it fit better the second time. Sometimes they will be prideful Tapodans. At other times they will seek the company of kids whose faces resemble ours at home. Or they may be drawn to popular youth cultures: urban hip hop, suburban prep, or pierced and tattooed Goth. Finding where you fit in the array of possibilities is maddening enough, as we should all remember from our own teenage years. This is no time for adoptive parents to insist that our kids squeeze into the exotic little personae we once created for them. Geir Follevåg, mindful of the legacy of Aryanism in Europe and of neo-Nazi sentiment in Norway, warns against the notion that adoptees are bound for life to a "natural," inborn cultural heritage. This biological determinism is, he argues, the basis of racism. He claims the right to be fully Norwegian, Asian features and all.

What we parents want most for our children, I assume, is happiness, security, and a confident self-acceptance. We help them attain that with genuine interest, handy resources, and access to their birth cultures. Yet we had best leave it to them to decide just who they will be when they grow up.

7

Raising Our Children in Isolation

Adopting a child should enrich my life, not turn it upside down. If I'm comfortable living where I do, he will be too. Happy parents, after all, have happy kids. If my family and friends and neighbors accept him as my son, he'll feel at home here. I don't see any reason to change my lifestyle or do anything as drastic as uproot myself.

In a course on writing the personal essay that I occasionally teach at the Loft Literary Center in Minneapolis, I ask the students to write three to five pages about an experience of race. Rather than simply pontificate about race, they are to ground their essays in their own lives. The white students, always the majority and often the totality of the class, generally choose their first encounter with a person of another color. One student I remember well—a white man about forty—insisted that he had nothing to write about. Because he grew up in an all-white town, went to an all-white college, lived in an all-white suburb, and worked in an all-white office, he explained, he had never had an experience of race. I paused and took a breath before responding: Segregation is the quintessential experience of race, more formative than any interracial encounter, whether friendly or awkward or hostile.

Dazed by the glare of his whiteness, this man honestly believed that his life had been racially neutral. Many adoptive parents share that illusion. While they expect their child to have a few qualms about being "different," they trust that a kindly acceptance will put those qualms to rest. As long as no one insults him or excludes him from group activities, all will be well. When people get to know him and recognize him as the adopted boy down the street, they will count him one of their own. And so these parents eagerly travel abroad to fetch their children or pick them up at the closest major airport and whisk them home to city enclaves or outlying suburbs or small towns or rural areas where race is of no concern because everyone is white.

Flash forward twenty-five or thirty years, and you get another perspective. Adult adoptees who have grown up in virtually all-white communities describe a common experience of race characterized by isolation, loneliness, confusion, and failed attempts to mask or change or deny their appearance in order to fit in. The Korean American filmmaker Jennifer Arndt, who interviewed adult adoptees in Seoul in *Crossing Chasms,* has a movie in progress about a Korean adoptee growing up in a small Midwestern town. My daughter and I heard her describe one funny but poignant slumber party scene in which the white girls apply their hairdo and makeup skills to their golden-skinned, almond-eyed, straight-haired friend, with clownlike results. Their failure to notice how ridiculous she looks is supposed to mean that they accept her as just like them. The notion of "acceptance" is itself belittling. It implies that treating someone unlike yourself as a human being is an act of generosity. And it only works one way. No one asks whether the adopted child accepts these different neighbors.

Moving from racial isolation to a more diverse environment can be a life-changing experience. Ami Nafzger grew up in rural Minnesota and had never met another Asian person until she entered Augsburg College in Minneapolis. One day she realized that an Asian woman was running after her through the campus. She wasn't sure whether to stop or flee. The woman had spotted her in the crowd and wanted to invite her to a meeting of the Asian American Students Association. Having passed among white people all her life, she was startled to be so quickly pegged as Asian American, yet she attended the meeting, got involved in the organization, and found herself with a changed identity and a new mission. After graduation she went to Korea to live for a while and met other adoptees with similar histories. At a meeting over coffee in March 1998 with Mihee Cho (Nathalie LeMoine of Belgium) and several other adoptees, Ami co-founded the organization GOA'L (Global Overseas Adoptees' Link), which helps returning adoptees locate housing, obtain visas, find jobs, search for birth families, and get to know each other. Her amazing trajectory from the only Asian in town to a pathbreaker for a worldwide population of adoptees is powerful testimony that the desire for community doesn't die off in isolation.

Ami told part of this story in a panel discussion at the 2002 KAAN Conference. My daughter and I approached her afterward to continue the conversation. When my daughter, then a student at Augsburg College, heard that Augsburg was where Ami first met another Asian, she burst out, "Augsburg? There aren't any Asians at Augsburg." She was used to watching Hmong boys break dance on the lunchroom floor at her urban high school. Augsburg, by contrast, felt overwhelmingly white. There are clearly degrees of racial isolation, depending on the perspective you bring.

At conferences, on e-mail lists, and in newsletters, adoptees who have grown up apart from people who resemble them urge parents to raise their children in racially diverse environments. Familiarity with people of other races spares them from the constricted view of the world that growing up in segregated white areas fosters—a view that discounts the value of their own heritage and either demeans them, declares them "special," or renders them invisible. Knowing people who have learned to dodge and deflect and defeat racism will equip them to meet challenges their parents have not likely faced. Best of all, in a setting of true and thorough diversity, racial boundaries blur and allow individuals to emerge. I remember the first time I rode a New York City subway with my daughter. It felt like the whole world had gathered on that train. The ride, from Flushing to Manhattan, was long enough to let us peruse the faces in the crowd. I found I couldn't place them all in the usual racial categories. There were white faces with African features, South Asians with skin darker than that of "black" African Americans . . . even this sentence is impossible to finish because the descriptors aren't ready at hand. (As a biracial student in my personal essay class wrote, "Your dictionary is too small for me.") And there *we* were, a young Asian woman and a middle-aged white woman traveling together, maybe confounding the people looking at us—or maybe not.

Diversity like that is not easy to come by, and I realize that the New York subway is not everyone's futuristic dream. We are mostly creatures of habit, birds of a feather flocking together, beings who seek comfort and avoid conflict. Even in the United States, where immigrants have been arriving since 1603, our instincts are not to jump into the mythical melting pot, but to preserve our distinctions by sticking with our own kind. The whites who take flight to the suburbs when others move in are not the only segregationists. Looking for an authentic Mexican restaurant in the Twin Cities? Try Concord Avenue in West St. Paul or Lake Street in Minneapolis. Curious about the rumor that Hmong immigrants are thriving as independent business people? Take a drive along University Avenue near the intersection of Dale. Want to worship in a Korean church on Sunday morning? Check the northern suburbs for the denomination of your choice. Larger cities than mine even mark Chinatown and Greektown and Little Italy on their maps.

Given this tendency, we can't really fault parents who object when adoptees advise them to relocate. If you have spent your life in a small town, the same one where your family has lived for generations, why should you have to uproot yourself to add a child to your family? Why should you give up your low-rate mortgage and your well-funded suburban school to move to the city where the houses are aging, the crime rate is higher, and the teachers are busy dealing with social problems? You know you wouldn't feel happy or safe there, so how could that be good for your child? Just keep in mind that he has the same instincts you do: to seek the comfort and safety of the familiar, which, as he grows up and becomes more self-aware, may mean faces less like yours and more like his. Remember, too, that he has traveled a great distance to fulfill your dreams of family. Your move across town or to a neighboring city or even to another state is a minor adjustment compared to the upheaval he has endured.

My older daughter was four years old and the younger just eighteen months when my marriage ended. I couldn't afford to stay in the house we had moved into the year before, and even the neighborhood was beyond my reach. Because Dad's departure and a second move so shortly after adoption were unnerving enough, I wanted to keep every other aspect of their lives stable. To my mind, that meant keeping them in the same preschool, staying close to familiar landmarks, shopping at the same grocery store, and having a lake within walking distance (not an unreasonable goal in Minnesota). After much searching, I found an affordable house about twenty blocks south in a cheaper but still "nice" neighborhood. Unfortunately it was a white neighborhood with only a smattering of darker faces. It has remained firmly white and even taken a disturbing turn toward economic exclusivity, as two-income professional couples buy the houses of retirees, add second stories to bungalows, and turn attics into master suites. The neighborhood drugstore and dry cleaner and convenience store have given way to coffee shops and gift shops. My daughters have watched this gentrification with the same consternation that some white residents felt about "blockbusting" back when African American families began buying real estate. The old neighborhood has gone to the dogs—"to the poodles," my daughter laments.

The Minneapolis school district's desegregation plan relies on specialized magnet schools to draw students from across the city. Ironically, the open-style elementary school my daughters attended turned out to be a popular choice for internationally adoptive families, so many of the children of color my girls met there also had white parents. School became a handy place to make friends with other adoptees. Their high school is one of the most diverse settings in the state of Minnesota. While the social groups at school were of the birds-of-a-feather variety and many of the extracurricular activities drew mostly white kids, the proximity of so many different people gave my daughters an ease with diversity that I still haven't learned. The names Taju and Pang don't elicit any more giggles than Katie and Mark. Girls in *hijab* don't draw their stares. Both my daughters started their higher educations at private liberal arts colleges, thinking the small size and close attention from faculty would suit them. Both missed the greater diversity of their high school and will no longer settle for nearly all-white environments.

I wish now that I had used our forced relocation to turn everything on end. I regret that I didn't look for a neighborhood that offered more diversity. It's dismaying to have to leave my neighborhood to see evidence of the new immigrant groups arriving in my city. Yet I have also entertained the possibility of moving the other way, back to very familiar territory, to my hometown in southern Minnesota. As my parents grew older and more infirm, I briefly considered resettling there to help them out. As a writer I can theoretically live anywhere and find some kind of work to support my writing habit. If I were alone, that might have been an attractive choice, but I would never ask my girls to be the token Asians at school in a town where anything out of the ordinary is described as "real different."

My daughters' chagrin with my extended family also made me think twice about this potential discomfort. Certainly the relatives "accept" them, but that doesn't mean the girls feel a family bond. When families are large and far flung and have little to connect them except childhood history and common genes, the favorite old stories and family resemblances get milked for all they're worth. Children who have no share in the family looks or history can't help but feel out of place at reunions. When they turn up at weddings and funerals, their difference from the family either makes them instantly recognizable ("Oh, you must be Cheri's little Korean girls!") or pegs them as strangers ("This pew is reserved for the family"). How often we have wished that some cousin would marry a person of another race and have children who don't immediately call the ancestors to mind. Until that happens, the family's monochromatic appearance feels unwelcoming.

But what if my parents' need for help had been critical, and they had no other resources to draw on? What if I had job security with a company that closed all its operations except for one in an all-white area and offered to transfer me there? Circumstances sometimes do compel us to rearrange our priorities. When that happens, we adoptive families have to come up with other schemes to mitigate the isolation: frequent visits to more diverse areas, vacations at ethnic culture camps, friends in cyberspace . . . Wherever we are, we must stop thinking of ourselves as white people who happen to have Tapodan children and reimagine ourselves as mixed-race families, not much different from those formed by interracial marriage. What kind of environment does our family need for everyone in it to thrive?

International adoption changes our families forever. Parents of teenagers who date only white classmates in the absence of other choices may ignore this possibility. They envision their families turning white again, with the Tapodan traits diluted in just a couple of generations. Yet as adoptees grow up and leave home and meet each other, they find that shared experience feeds other attractions. Our grandchildren may look as Tapodan as our children. As they seek out and find comfort in diversity, our kids may well find mates of other colors. Ponder the example of Camilla Pedersen, Korean born, raised in Norway, married to a man from India, living in the United States. In time, our families could look like the passengers on the New York subway. We would be wise to behave as if they already do.

8

Judging Our Country Superior

I really love my country, and I want my daughter to be as proud and patriotic as I am. I remind her often how lucky she is to live here, so she won't forget that not everyone in the world has it this good. Poor, underdeveloped Tapoda was no place for an intelligent, talented girl like her. Why, the Tapodans keep women oppressed. The whole country looks run-down and dirty, and they eat the most awful things there.

Back when we imagined the children we would someday bear, we took for granted that they would be little Belgians or Aussies or Swiss like us. Born into citizenship, they would inherit our features and look the part, primed to embody the habits and values our country holds dear. When we first thought about adopting internationally, we wondered whether this last expectation was still reasonable: raised as one of us, would an adopted child still feel allegiance to Tapoda?

Shortly after my husband and I told my parents that we had applied to adopt a baby from Korea, my dad expressed his concern to my sister. "What if she grows up and goes back to Korea?" he asked. My sister reassured him: "This will be her home. If she grows up here, she'll be an American." If this child was to be ours in every way, she would, of course, share our national identity. Yet because my husband was a Dutch immigrant and I am a third-generation Danish American, there was no question that she would be raised, as we were, with an appreciation for her ethnicity. Her Korean heritage wouldn't diminish her American identity, but enhance her sense of possibility as a citizen of the world.

Since then, I have been dismayed to learn that some parents equate adoption with metamorphosis. Once the child "comes home," a phrase that suggests she has been away in some place where she doesn't belong, she takes on the identity and heritage of her adoptive family. Tapoda is the discarded cocoon, no longer of any use. If the parents aren't impressed with their trip to Tapoda or what they hear about its culture—if it strikes them as odd or primitive—they take pride in the wonderful gift of nationality they have given their child. They will raise her to be as proud of her citizenship as they are to have been born in their clean and decent and civilized country.

I first encountered this type of thinking in Sweden decades ago, even before I imagined myself adopting. At a party in a daycare center, I met a blonde woman with a dark-skinned child on her lap. When she heard that I was American, she told me with great pride about the extralegal efforts she had gone to in order to bring a black child from the United States to Sweden. What a lucky girl, she continued, to be growing up in a country where everyone is equal and well cared for, instead of in that horrid ghetto. As we talked, it became apparent that the mother knew nothing about the vitality of African American culture and had never questioned the superiority of her own culture. The "guest workers" and refugees who would put Swedish norms and Swedes' tolerance of outsiders to the test were just beginning to arrive.

Certainly not all parents, but still far too many, display their ethnocentrism in the process of adopting. They practice what Barbara Melosh, the author of *Strangers and Kin: The American Way of Adoption,* calls "petulant entitlement." She cites the example of an American seeking to adopt from a Romanian orphanage who argued that her citizenship in a wealthy country made her the stronger contender for a child whose birth parents had come to reclaim him. A controversy still raging, at this writing, in the state of Andhra Pradesh, India, has pitted local child welfare advocates against prospective parents in the United States. Revelations that some children had not been legally relinquished put a temporary stop to international placements until the remaining children's status could be confirmed. Some of the parents left waiting have reacted with an impatience that shows an arrogant disregard for Indian families and for the Indian state's right to establish its own child welfare principles. Arrogance is heard as well in the persistent rumors that Korea might "close up" as a source of adoptable children. The day that no Korean child needs to be placed abroad should be a day of celebration.

No matter how you plan to raise your child, you will, immediately after her arrival, encounter fellow citizens of your country eager to tell you how lucky she is to be growing up there. These reminders of her good fortune will never cease. They arise out of a self-assured nationalism that without question ranks your country as better than her birthplace. The people who make these comments intend them as a welcome, a kindness bestowed on your child to help her feel as lucky and privileged as they believe her to be. She, however, hears the subtext: that she is alien and inferior, ever to be singled out of the crowd as a foreigner who doesn't really belong.

Without the frequent reminders of her foreignness, she too might be content to settle in as a full citizen. If she were treated exactly like a native, she might take for granted that the beliefs and habits and mores that govern her life, like yours, are natural and normal and universal. But she comes from somewhere else, and she will eventually grow curious about that place. Political refugees, economic migrants, and other immigrants have memories, fond or frightening, of the countries they left behind. Even if compelled to leave home, they have made the decision to seek asylum or residence or citizenship in your country. Your child had no choice, and unless she was older at the time of adoption, she has no memory of her birthplace. What if it had been up to her? she wonders. Would she have chosen this country or some other, and how would it feel not to be uprooted at all, but to be a citizen of Tapoda? This is, of course, a two-pronged question: How does the average Tapodan live? And would that way of life be available to me, given the circumstances I was born into? She will spin her answer to those questions out of fact and fantasy, depending to some extent on the information you offer and the attitude you convey.

In the spring of 2003 my daughter and I attended a conference in Copenhagen on "The Meaning of Roots: Ethnic Identity and Biological Heritage," sponsored by Koreaklubben, the Danish association of Korean adopt-

Cheri Register

ees. By the accents with which the participants spoke English, the common language of the conference, we could tell pretty quickly that they had gathered from several European countries. Though they looked Korean in coloring and facial features, there were telling differences in demeanor. The academic work I used to do in Scandinavia taught me to distinguish the stiff, upright posture of the Norwegians from the casualness and ready humor of the Danes. When one of the participants cited statistics from memory to bolster his argument, I thought to myself, "Just like a Swede." Growing up where they did had stamped these adoptees with the set of traits we sometimes label "national character." My other daughter, too, has observed these national traits in the subculture of adoptees living in Seoul. "I met two guys from the Netherlands yesterday," she wrote once. "I know this is going to sound weird, but they remind me of Dad."

National identity is a more complicated matter. A major theme of the conference was whether it is healthier for adoptees to be content with the identity conferred on them by adoption or to engage in what the academics in attendance called "root-seeking behavior." Several speakers talked about how difficult this issue is, that it's not simply a personal choice, but depends on others' perceptions. Since most of their parents believed that assimilation and color blindness were the best policies, the national identity they wore at home was that of the European country where they lived. Out on the street, however, this identity was always in question. Even those who wanted to think of themselves as native were reminded again and again—by kindly assumptions, by intrusive questions, by racist comments—that they weren't who they thought they were.

Charlotte Yong San Gullach of Denmark listed three categories of questions that widen the gap between adoptees and their Danish-born peers:

1. The origin question: "Where do you come from?" (Meaning: You don't belong here.)

2. The gratitude question: "Aren't you grateful that you came to Denmark?" (Meaning: You're not equal to me.)

3. The definition question: "What race are you?" (Meaning: You're not my type.)

The adoptees' self-perceptions fall somewhere between their adoptive identity and their birth identity, in the realm of lucky foreigner, with a family to bestow the privilege of honorary European. But with its undertone of "inferior by birth," lucky foreigner is not a comfortable identity.

In the Swedish book *Mariamma,* by the Indian adoptee Anna Rosenqvist with her friend Christina Åsbäck, Rosenqvist offers this clever, satirical take on what it's like to be brown-skinned in Sweden: "You should get a stamp on your arm when you come to the land of order and cleanliness. For example, 'Made in India,' so people don't have to wonder. The upper part of the question mark gets eliminated, so only the period remains. This would simultaneously create a new job opportunity in the land of information, and that's not so dumb, is it? Not everybody, you know, can work informing about one thing and the other all day long. You can certainly use your hands for something concrete instead, and why not to manufacture stamp pads? Swedish handmade stamp pads that can compete with the Dala horse itself on the shelf of souvenirs from Sweden."

Most of the European countries that adopt internationally have long histories of homogeneity and have experienced significant immigration from other parts of the world only since the 1970s. Even two or three generations after immigration, the population of these countries is clearly divisible into natives and foreigners. A corresponding rise in racism makes life extra difficult for those who don't look native. It's not surprising that some adoptees empathize and identify with the immigrants, despite growing up in the intimacy of a native family. This affinity troubles their parents, especially those skeptical of the influence of foreigners on their homeland's traditions. They don't want the precious gift of nationality they have given their children to be rejected. Other adoptees avoid associating with apparent foreigners to keep their national identity unchallenged. Jan (Dae-won) Wenger of Dongari, an organization for Korean adoptees in Switzerland, told *Korean Quarterly* how hard it is to reach those who insist on being "200% Swiss." There is not much middle ground.

National identity is not such an either-or matter in the United Kingdom, with its large communities drawn from former colonies of the British Empire. Nor is it so in the United States, which claims a proud history as a nation of immigrants. Many Americans bear dual-heritage identities even three or four generations after immigration. An adoptee raised in a dual-heritage family as Brigid Murphy or Leda Papadopolos or Miriam Goldstein not only becomes American, but takes on her family's ethnicity as well. Although I cherish my daughters' Korean identities, I know I have unwittingly raised them with Scandinavian American behavioral traits. Much of this assimilation happens naturally because of who and how we parents are. But if the family's ethnicity is only a vague remnant of the ancestral culture, bearing it as an identity feels absurd. I remember one Minnesota adoptee shaking her head as she told about her mother's insistence that she was no longer Korean, but Norwegian. How could she be Norwegian, she wondered, if she had never even been to Norway? These multiple identities easily confound small children. A young man I know used to call himself one-quarter Korean, one-quarter Jewish, one-quarter American, and one-quarter "whatever Dad is."

A more viable identity for those adopted to the United States might be that of the larger racial or cultural group they resemble: Latino or Asian American or African American or whatever. Those wide umbrellas shade people of many national origins, both new immigrants and some with a long heritage here. They offer more room for self-definition than the narrower Tapodan.

Since September 11, 2001, being American has become a question not only of nationality or citizenship, but also of allegiance or patriotism. A new skepticism toward immigrants and a foreign policy that puts American interests ahead of all others have made it still more challenging for international adoptees to simply *be* American. What happens when the citizens of Tapoda look askance at American behavior in the world or protest the impact of American culture on their country? What if Tapoda's national interests come into conflict with U.S. foreign policy? American history shows that we don't always handle these conflicts well. During World War I, German Americans were ordered to give up German-language newspapers, church services, even conversation, or face punishment. During World War II, American citizens of Japanese descent who lived on the U.S. mainland were deprived of their property and sent away to internment camps. Adoptees aware of this history may not feel the glow of American patriotism that their white, native-born parents wish for them. I like the way Martha Vickery, the editor of *Korean Quarterly,* resolves the tension: "I love my country, but cautiously, like the love between lifelong friends whose faults and shortcomings you know only too well." That's the kind of responsible patriotism I would happily nurture in my children.

When planes began flying again after September 11, I was among the first passengers. My publisher, based in Manhattan, had continued to make arrangements for a book tour on the West Coast, and I felt I ought to honor that commitment. On the flight out, all the way up the Pacific Coast, and on the flight back, the sky was absolutely clear. I saw Bryce Canyon, the Grand Canyon, all the peaks from Shasta to Baker, the Bitterroots and the Mission Range, the jagged outlines of the Fort Peck Reservoir, the North Dakota Badlands, and the whole stretch of prairie from there to Minneapolis. I was awestruck. "America the Beautiful" played in my mind as I peered out the plane window and watched this vast, sparsely inhabited landscape slide by. It was reassuring to see it still there, from the "purple mountains' majesty" to the "amber waves of grain." I wanted my daughters to know the glory of that landscape, though much was lost in the telling.

I often think about what I treasure most in my American heritage. What legacy do I want to pass on to my daughters? The list ranges widely, from the New England Transcendentalists to the flowering of multicultural literature in the late twentieth century; from the Federalist Papers to Martin Luther King's "Letter from Birmingham Jail"; from the blues, a plaintive music born of poverty and oppression, to John Philip Sousa's upbeat parade marches; from the Bill of Rights to the grass-roots populism those amendments protect; from maple syrup to popcorn. Yet I know that my girls' lists might be different. Their perception of what it means to be American is determined by their age and generation, their urban upbringing, their education, and their experience of race and ethnicity. We Americans treasure our privacy and our freedom of movement, yet our internationally adopted children's privacy is continually intruded upon by questions calling them to account for their presence here.

To figure out my American identity, I returned to my roots. I majored in Scandinavian languages and literatures and continued on to a Ph.D. I traveled to Scandinavia frequently. Even on our recent trip to Copenhagen, I took two days before the conference to engage in my own "root-seeking behavior." I dragged my poor daughter out in a heavy, wet spring snowfall to catch the bus to Gundsømagle, the little town near the Roskilde Fjord where my grandmother grew up. Since my last visit twenty-five years earlier, a fire in the Gundsømagle church had burned away layers of lime wash on the walls and revealed murals painted early in the twelfth century. Standing inside that church, I felt deeply rooted, imagining some ancestor of mine in that same spot nearly a millennium ago. I want my daughters to feel that rootedness, too, wherever it happens.

Just as my dad conjectured, my older daughter *did* grow up and go back to Korea to experience life in her birth country and figure out just what a mix of national character and identity she is. The many adoptees she has met there have come back for the same reasons. A few grew up as she did, with some attempts to instill a Korean identity, but most come from homes where Korea was rarely mentioned. Some have returned over their parents' objections or to their parents' bewilderment. The people who used to comment on how lucky my children are recite a new line now: "Oh, how nice of you to let her do that." Others assume she has gone to Korea to stay, perhaps to live with her birth family. They don't realize that people raised outside their birthplace, even the children of emigrant families, don't slip easily back into the mold.

Kari Ruth returned from her sojourn in Korea with newfound wisdom that she shared with *Korean Quarterly:* "I didn't find information about my birth or background on this trip. I didn't find answers to my questions about identity. I didn't find an inherent connection with my birth country or its people. Those weren't my expectations. I did rediscover something I wasn't expecting, though— courage. I saw it in the other AK's [adopted Koreans] I met who are here studying, working or trying to carve out a space for themselves here in Korea. . . . Some people view the AK's who return to Korea as lost souls who have come home to roost. I didn't see people who should be pitied. I saw some of the strongest people I will ever know who had the courage to return and stand tall and proud while trying to balance the uneven and often contradictory aspects of their lives."

Ruth's image of courageous returned adoptees suggests another identity available to our children besides Tapodan or "whatever Dad is." At the Copenhagen conference, Tobias Hübinette proposed a third way: to identify not with a country, but with a community of exiles—a diaspora of international adoptees. The hundreds of thousands of children of various countries sent abroad for adoption from the 1950s on into an indefinite future are a citizenry unto themselves, people who share the experience of involuntary displacement from one family to another and one country to another. Their identity depends on the most truthful, meaningful answers they can find to those persistent questions, "Where are you from?" and "What are you?" Whether they name our country or their birthplace or say, "I'm an international adoptee," the best we can wish for them is a firm sense of belonging.

9

Believing Adoption Saves Souls

I *believe that God has a direct hand in adoption.
I explain to my son that God meant him to be
ours all along, but he just happened to be born in the wrong
place. God guided us all the way to Tapoda to find him.
We are so grateful that our faith was strong enough to over-
come all the obstacles thrown in our way by social workers
and government bureaucrats. It was, after all, God's will
that he be rescued and raised by believers.*

How eagerly we want to believe, when we finally hold that tiny referral photo in our hands, that this is indeed *the* child, *our* child, the one best suited to our family. We'd like to think that some larger force—God, Fate, the Red Thread, Lady Luck—drew our attention to that particular face on the Internet or guided the social worker or government official to pull our file out of the stack when that particular case history turned up. The notion that an ordinary human being made a rational yet arbitrary decision to match this child with us can't account for the waves of emotion the photo sets loose. But what if, instead of your beloved child, you *should* have been assigned the next child, the one who went to Perth or Lausanne or Tenafly? Could God possibly bungle it? No, no, we insist. Whatever happens was meant to be.

After the child arrives, we stay alert to signals that he is truly ours: the way he knits his eyebrows just like Grandpa; the way she sleeps with her knees tucked under her and her little butt pushed up, just like the cousins born into the family; the mellow, unruffled personality just like his uncle's. Watching for a family resemblance, as long as it's not an illusion that obscures his actual traits, is not a bad way to bond with a new child. It's certainly better than focusing on disappointments and unfamiliar habits that peg him as too alien to be a complete member of the family. The similarities we identify don't necessarily depend on a cosmic explanation. We make friends, too, by highlighting the qualities we share. That doesn't mean that our coming together as friends is anything more than coincidence. Surely there are other folks scattered about the world whom we would like just as much if we happened to meet them. Whenever I'd venture too far in claiming that my kids were the most suitable picks of the bunch, they would ask, "What if you had gotten Anne or Katie instead?" Of course I would love them as much and find just as many traits to bind them to me. That I can't deny.

Many Christians look to the Bible for evidence that adoption is divinely ordained. God himself, they say, was an adoptive parent whose only son was born to Mary and Joseph, an earthly couple. (Actually Mary's impregnation by the Holy Spirit is more like a case of surrogacy.) Evangelical Christians liken baptism and born-again experiences to an adoption that formalizes the relationship with God as heavenly father. Christians, Jews, and Muslims share the story of Moses' adoption by the Pharaoh's daughter, who found him in a basket in the reeds where his mother had hidden him to protect him from the Pharaoh's edict that all Hebrew male babies be killed. This is one of my favorite Bible stories, especially the clever part where Miriam, Moses' sister, brings their mother to the Pharaoh's daughter to serve as wet nurse. I even bought Warwick Hutton's picture book, *Moses in the Bulrushes,* for my daughter's fourth birthday in the hope that she would identify her own story with this one.

When we try to apply these Biblical examples to our mortal lives, however, the parallels aren't so neat. God allowed Christ to be sacrificed for the salvation of humanity. Which of us is willing to surrender our child? Or did the birth parents perform a Godlike act by relinquishing their child for adoption? Who, exactly, is being saved? Moses' upbringing in Pharaoh's household didn't turn him into an Egyptian, but equipped him to lead the Israelites out of bondage in Egypt. Who among our children will lead the exodus back to Tapoda? Are we ready for that?

Some parents treat the cliché "a match made in heaven" as a religious certainty. A few adoption agencies, too, claim that God alone chooses which child to place with which parents, no accidents or coincidences involved. On an Internet list, I read about a couple who plan to tell their daughter that God arranged for her to be born in China to test their fitness as parents, to see if they loved her enough to go all the way to China to fetch her. Meanwhile, her soul sat up in heaven watching them—her "real" parents—and cheering them on. The birth parents have barely a walk-on role in this tale.

I have problems with a theology of God-as-Micromanager. Why would a just and loving God routinely take children away from poor parents in struggling countries and hand them over to people of greater wealth? Wouldn't God instead prevent untimely births and reduce the suffering that abandonment and displacement afflict on both birth parents and children? How can we presume to know that God personally moves each and every child from one spot on the globe to another? Who among us has read the adoption master plan? Is it still God's will if strings are pulled, laws evaded, and bribes paid to make the adoption happen? That's a bit like excusing mistakes with "The devil made me do it." This theology absolves us human beings of responsibility for the conditions that fuel international adoption, and it's ethnocentric besides. Does God truly love us more than the Tapodans?

Of course not all devout parents believe so literally that God alone is the instrumental force behind adoption. Many see no lack of faith in acknowledging the political conditions, the economic realities, the human efforts that make adoption happen the way it does. They may nevertheless treat the outcome as cause for divine rejoicing. Their child, born to parents of no faith or a different faith, has come to a family that worships God in the one way they consider right and true. Adoption, then, is a route to salvation.

People of Christian faith have, of course, played major roles in establishing international adoption. When Henry and Bertha Holt brought children out of war-torn Korea in the 1950s, they believed God had called them to that mission. Henry Holt traced the call to the prophecy in Isaiah 43:5 and 6. The Korean orphans were "seed from the East" to be planted in Western, Christian soil. Nowadays, this notion has an imperialistic ring, but in the aftermath of that war it made some sense. The first children the Holts placed were mainly mixed-race offspring of foreign military personnel. Korea did not claim these children as its own because their fathers, through whom ancestry is traced in a patrilineal culture, were not Korean. International adoption was, from the Korean vantage point, a repatriation that merged fairly easily with the Holts' intentions. There was no contest of religious wills, since Confucian Buddhists protected the purity of family bloodlines and had no inclination to convert others in the way the Christians did.

The native-run orphanages and child welfare agencies that sprang up in Korea and other countries were also largely Christian in origin. The one responsible for my children was founded by a Korean Methodist layman who, following the admonition in the Gospels, took on a personal ministry to care for widows and orphans. Placing children abroad was not his first intent, but became a solution to the magnitude of the need. International adoption took hold in India in the state of Kerala, which has been populated by Christians since the first century A.D.

The major South Asian religions, Hinduism and Islam, rarely place children for adoption outside the faith. Orphanages run by Catholic religious orders have housed the children adopted from Vietnam and Latin American countries. Today, too, in both the sending and the receiving countries, many of the agencies overseeing international adoption identify themselves by denomination or simply as Christian.

The Christian call to care for orphans has motivated parents as well, especially in the earlier days when there were enough domestically born infants available to meet the needs of infertile couples. Parents with seemingly complete families took in additional children regardless of race as a charitable response to homelessness. Slogans like "Every child deserves a home" and "Make room for one more" encouraged church members to do this kind deed. Most of these children, now middle-aged, thrived in ways they never would have in orphanages or on the street. At best, genuine familial love replaced the charitable intentions that brought them to their families. Yet there is just enough discontent in this group to serve as a lesson for the rest of us. I have heard adoptees talk of how it feels to be treated as a perpetual charity case. Reminded frequently of the conditions they came from, they feel worthy of love only if they are sufficiently grateful for their rescue.

A newer generation of parents is, like those early families, motivated to adopt by Christian faith, but their charity seems more like a means of evangelism. Adoption, in their eyes, rescues children not only from abject social conditions, but also from false beliefs and likely damnation. "Bringing God's children home" assures their conversion to Christianity. When adoption is equated with the saving of souls, however, almost any means to that end can be justified. If international adoption is to be conducted in an ethical, egalitarian, and nonracist manner, claims of religious righteousness must be dropped.

None of this history should be read as proof that Christianity is a superior religion in its charity for the poor, its love of children, or its concern for their spiritual welfare. Even evangelical Christian parents who have adopted from China, for example, testify to the tender care bestowed in some state-run orphanages by non-Christian personnel. Yet too many parents leap to the conclusion that Christians care the most. Few of us are educated enough in the world's many faiths and belief systems to make judgments about how they manage the common good, keep community life safe and orderly, and foster the well-being of children. They may proceed in ways different from the Christian practice of charity, which is more palliative than preventive, and emphasize shoring up the whole rather than tending to its parts. They may, for example, see lines of ancestry as inviolable and work to keep them from being ruptured. They may see their religious community as geographically or ethnically finite and grieve the loss of any child transported beyond those boundaries. Or they may believe that *their* faith is superior and bemoan the fate of children adopted by nonbelievers.

We are also shamefully uneducated about adoption practices in the sending countries. In the book *Wanting a Daughter, Needing a Son,* Kay Ann Johnson, a professor of Asian Studies, reveals that Chinese people are in fact quite willing to adopt abandoned children, especially girls, but are curtailed by the same population control policies that drive birth parents to abandonment. In several countries, international adoption has taken on a momentum that discourages domestic adoption. The higher fees charged to foreigners bring in the revenue needed to maintain orphanages and other social services. Even if Tapodans do indeed resist adoption, we should try to understand why, and how this attitude relates to the preservation of the whole community, rather than deem their beliefs less humane than our own. Just as we acknowledge that our children have genetic relatives elsewhere in the world and another country and culture to show respect for, we must honor the possibility that their genetic family lives by a belief system different from ours.

The term *belief system* sounds more technological than human for the aspect of culture I have in mind: what people believe about the origin and purpose of life, the relationship between human action and natural phenomena, and the meaning of suffering and death. I would use the word *religion* for the stature it confers if it didn't imply formal creeds and institutions of worship and belief in a personal God. I want a better word than the vague *spirituality* or the reductive *mythology* or the judgmental *superstitions* or the belittling *customs*. No matter which word we use, the Tapodans' beliefs are as vital to them as ours are to us, and they are central to our children's ethnic heritage. A Korean American admonished me one time, "Remember, even Korean Christians are Confucian." It would be wise, in other words, to learn what that means and not assume too much.

Adoptive parents are, of course, as entitled as reproducing parents to raise our children in the family's faith, whatever it might be. Worshiping together, conducting religious rituals, observing religious holidays, and being part of a faith community are typical family practices that strengthen "the ties that bind." Adopted children are as entitled as birth children to the excitement of a First Communion or a Bar or Bat Mitzvah or a Coming of Age ceremony. And adolescents of all faiths are entitled to follow their natures and question the givens of their religious upbringing. Neither of my daughters chose to be confirmed at fifteen in the Presbyterian church I still attend. The whiteness and advanced age of the congregation made them wonder if there weren't other ways of understanding life's purpose that resonated better with their lives. (Ironically, that church is enjoying an influx of young families and West African immigrants, and I hear people conversing in Korean at the Sunday coffee hour.) I'm proud of my daughters' honesty. I had balked at Lutheran confirmation myself because I wanted to satisfy my curiosity about other religions, but I went through the ceremony with my fingers crossed so that the magic I expected to happen wouldn't take. I also trust that life will bring my daughters, as it has me, to a reckoning with their own deepest selves and whatever they choose to call the power beyond them.

A small child might welcome the security in a story that God chose him out of all the children in the world and placed him in this, his rightful, family. But imagine how that notion can gnaw at an adolescent who is beginning to ponder the meaning of his existence. What comfort will he find in a religion that requires him to be taken away from his birth parents so that God can bestow the blessing of his presence on his adoptive family and save his soul besides? "Were my birth parents bad?" he wonders. "Will they go to hell if I don't find them and save them too? If I'm their child, I must be just as bad. Why did God choose to save me and not the kids left behind in

Tapoda? Are my parents really and truly my only path to righteousness? Then how can I ever get along on my own if my parents hold the keys to heaven? How can I trust my judgment? What if being Tapodan means that I can't hear the will of God the way they do?"

Then suppose he meets some actual Tapodans or travels to Tapoda to check it out. The Tapodan people don't act the way he would expect nonbelievers to act. They are decent, humane, welcoming, happy, loving people. "Can they be so wrong?" he wonders. "It doesn't seem like they want to hurt me or brainwash me or lead me astray. And what about the beautiful places of worship they've built and preserved for centuries? If it's all idolatry, why does walking inside make you feel so calm, as if you're in the presence of something holy? How can I be sure that my parents are closer to God than these people? What gives them sole rights to the truth? What if this has all been a hoax to keep me from searching for my roots?" That last thought can strain family ties to the breaking point.

Yes, I know that extending Christ's promise of salvation to others is foundational to Christianity. One of the first verses we memorized in my Lutheran Sunday School was Matthew 28:19: "Go ye therefore and make disciples of all nations, baptizing them in the name of the Father, the Son, and the Holy Ghost." Too often, though, that charge has been enforced by unholy military power or subverted to commercial and political ends that don't improve the recipients' lot. I have no doubt that parents who believe God makes all the decisions in adoption are motivated by the joy and comfort they find in their faith. The desire to share good news and be of help is instinctual in all of us. I wouldn't write this book if I didn't have that instinct myself. But sharing good news implies that someone is listening and pondering and evaluating. Babies and young children don't have that capacity. Evangelism is a matter best left to consenting adults.

10

Appropriating Our Children's Heritage

International adoption is such a fascinating multicultural adventure. Now that I have a Tapodan child, we'll be welcome at all the Tapodan ethnic events. I look forward to making a whole new set of friends—intriguing friends with life stories more exciting than mine. I'll ask them to teach me Tapodan cooking and help me find Tapodan furniture and art to redecorate my house. My daughter will hardly know she's left Tapoda. Our whole family will be Tapodan now.

I saved this pitfall for last because I'm still teetering on its edge. Count me among the parents who yearn to partake of all the splendor the world has to offer. We hate to miss any of the foreign movies that come to town, and we take pride in not always having to read the subtitles. We enjoy trying new flavors at ethnic restaurants and adding bolder spices to our kitchen supply. We tune our car radios to ethnic stations and delight in the cadences without a clue about the words. We shop at global markets that return profits to indigenous handicraft guilds and aren't ashamed to display our fleshy Caucasian hips in Guatemalan stripes. We clap along—sometimes off beat—to African rhythms and even venture a few dance steps. Our enthusiasm for life is fed by humanity's beautiful diversity. We dream of a world where all cultures are honored and allowed to prevail, unthreatened by economic or military domination. We even catch ourselves humming along with the Coke song—we *would* like the world to sing in perfect harmony—until we remember that Coca-Cola has the world drinking in unison for a hefty profit.

Back in the 1960s, in the midst of civil rights movements and anticolonial struggles for independence, white people who favored racial and cultural equality opened their families to homeless children regardless of race in the belief that racial barriers were crumbling. Canadian families adopted Native, or First Nations, children, and white Americans became the parents of African American, American Indian, and biracial children. (Australia has a different history of transracial "adoption." Indigenous children were removed from their families and placed in white homes in accordance with a long-running government policy of forced assimilation.) Some of these families were large, included children of several origins, and joyfully called themselves a "mini United Nations." They saw themselves as harbingers of a new society no longer divided by race, a society where love and companionship and neighborliness knew no cultural barriers.

What a shock these parents felt when in 1972 the National Council of Black Social Workers in the United States denounced transracial adoption as "cultural genocide." At about the same time, Native American tribes asserted their authority over the placement of orphaned or abandoned children. Child welfare policies that removed children from allegedly incompetent parents also came under scrutiny for inherent racism. (In Australia members of "the Stolen Generation" sought to end the relocation of indigenous children.) Instead of admiration for their large-heartedness and lack of bigotry, white parents of black and Indian children met vilification for draining the lifeblood from the very communities with which they had sought to make common cause.

When my husband and I decided to adopt in 1980, we knew how complicated it would be to claim an African American or Native American child as our own. Yet we attributed the controversy about transracial adoption to the particular history of slavery and genocide in the United States and didn't apply it to international adoption. Though we never sought to adopt internationally for its own sake, adoption from Korea looked like a safe, efficient, and ethically sound possibility, and so we embraced it. I still had some questions and anticipated some difficulty, but I also welcomed the chance to inscribe my family in the emerging global community. In conversations with like-minded parents, we shared our excitement at the adventure we had embarked on. Our multicultural families just might transform the world.

We looked forward to being transformed ourselves by the "color" our children would bring to our humdrum domestic lives. I was reminded of this expectation when I heard the new father of a Russian son extol the cultural benefits of international adoption. His son, he said, brought a rich cultural heritage along with him to the United States, a country that has no culture. Culture, presumably, means embroidered shirts and knee-high boots, not T-shirts and jeans; lively balalaika music, not jazz or country and western; onion-domed architecture, not big-box stores with massive parking lots; borscht, not Campbell's soup. Like white people who presume to have no race, white Americans seldom think of their ways as "ethnic." And so we latch on to "exotic" tastes and habits and artifacts to dress up our lives, which we believe to be basic and ordinary.

The issue of cultural *appropriation,* if not cultural genocide, lurks in international adoption, but living at a distance from the people who might object, prospective parents don't hear enough nay-saying to be discouraged. Instead, the vision of global harmony and a lush multiculturalism still governs the choices of some adopting parents, who believe that their love for Tapodan children will help to right the balance between their own wealthy countries and disadvantaged Tapoda. When their xenophobic compatriots see these beautiful Tapodan children mingling with their own, maybe they, too, will open their hearts to the world. And is there any better evidence of the parents' broad-mindedness than a child of another origin? They have dared to stretch their boundaries even within the intimacy of family life. Their families won't be private havens, but public demonstrations of their social and political will. With a Tapodan child in hand, they will, they expect, be welcomed into ethnic gatherings of *any* variety.

Some parents immerse themselves in Tapodan culture, eager to master it and make it their own. Doing Tapodan things together becomes their family's bonding mechanism, like playing catch or dressing in mother-daughter outfits. They refurnish their homes, change their diet and their place of worship, slap Tapodan stickers on their cars, and fill their bookshelves with Tapodan literature and their CD stands with Tapodan music. If there is an immigrant community nearby, they make it their second home, not only to learn about Tapodan culture, but also to find Tapodans who will adopt their family in return.

The current wisdom in adoption circles encourages as much direct contact with the child's culture of origin as feasible. We should stop short, however, of feeling entitled to the community's blessings. The presence of Tapodan children in our homes doesn't transform us into honorary Tapodans, no matter what polite Tapodans say to our faces. A cold shoulder or mere indifference is not in itself a charge of cultural genocide, but we should heed these signs nevertheless and tread cautiously. A white person's multicultural dream may be a Tapodan's neocolonial nightmare. History gives them good reason to mistrust the intentions of enthusiastic Westerners, especially ones who want their children. Kindness should be received gratefully, not simply expected.

Cultural appropriation rears its head where we least expect it: in our relationships with the children on whose behalf we have crossed these boundaries. How many of us have bargained with reluctant children to get them to a Tapodan event or simply used our superior strength and authority to force them into the car? We tell them, and ourselves, that we're doing this for their good, that they will thank us for it someday, and maybe they will. But how often do we interrupt our enjoyment of Tapodan culture to ask ourselves, or them, why they balk? Maybe they see through our illusions of welcome and sense that the Tapodans are embarrassed or offended by international adoption. They feel far more acutely than we do the disparity between themselves and the "real" Tapodans, as some adoptees put it. Negotiating a relationship with the birth culture they have been displaced from is more complicated and emotionally laden than it is for us parents, who rarely question our status as natives of our own culture. Our ease with Tapodan matters may look to them like cultural appropriation, like we have blithely scooped up for ourselves what they have lost.

These days, with a daughter living in Korea, I often think back to a well-intended moment in her childhood. On a trip to Los Angeles, we were staying with a high school friend of mine in a suburb above the city. When she offered us a tour of L.A. and asked what we would like to see, I answered immediately, "Koreatown." My kids might have preferred the beach or Universal Studios, but I chose something good for us: the opportunity to mingle in the largest Korean community in the United States, where they would see block after block of people who looked like them. Besides, I was hungry for *bi bim bop.* I also wanted my Scandinavian American friend to understand that adopting children from another country meant embracing their heritage as well.

We parked in front of a row of Korean-named appliance stores and insurance companies across the street from the side entrance to an enclosed shopping mall. Inside we passed clothing and jewelry stores in our search for a place to eat lunch. The aroma of kimchee and soy sauce led us to a food court on the lower level. My friend picked at her lunch a little skeptically, and I blamed that on her isolation up there in the white hills. I felt entirely comfortable, and proud of that, watching all the Asian people stream by. As accustomed as I am to the sight of my daughters, I often forget that I don't look like them. Sitting in a Koreatown mall just months before the Rodney King beating and the burning and looting that damaged the neighborhood, it barely occurred to me to feel like an intruder.

After my twelve-year-old daughter had eaten, she asked if she could go window shopping while the rest of us dawdled over our lunches. Of course I said yes. I figured she wanted to test how it felt to blend into the crowd, and I was happy to oblige. I probably even explained all that to my friend. Only later did I realize what blending into the crowd required. It meant leaving me behind so my white presence wouldn't give away who she really was.

That little incident in Koreatown has been an enduring lesson. It's my job to introduce my children to Korean culture, to ease their access to Korea and Korean communities, but then I had best get out of the way. The Indian British sociologist David Woodger warns parents against setting ourselves up as experts on our children's birth cultures. Our good intentions can backfire by intimidating our children and limiting their space to explore the culture and claim it as theirs. If I insist on being the mediator, the person who teaches and interprets the culture to my daughters as I, an enthusiastic outsider, perceive it, I have appropriated it for myself. Korean culture is *their* heritage, not mine. It is theirs to experience directly, to encounter on their own terms, with all the longing and sorrow it arouses in them. If there are times when they'd rather just leave it alone, I should cool my heels and read *Korean Quarterly* in silence—or make kale soup and *aebleskiver* to remind myself that I have a heritage of my own. In a quarter century of adoptive family life, I haven't yet turned Korean.

As I said, I'm still teetering on the edge of this pitfall. I find the lines between a supportive interest and cultural appropriation hard to detect sometimes. My daughters and I have all wanted to learn the Korean language, but opportunities to do so are rare where we live. One daughter took a semester of language at the University of Minnesota, then went to Korea to continue. The other daughter and I signed up for a weekly evening class taught by a native speaker at an international center where we could also choose Somali or Spanish or Arabic or Hmong. I had three good reasons for taking this class. First, I was about to visit my daughter in Korea. On my two previous trips, I felt at a loss with no language skills. I don't like to travel at the mercy of others or to be the Ugly American who expects everyone to speak English. Second, I enjoy learning languages and had long intended to study a non-Indo-European language to see what it's like to get away from familiar syntax and cognate words. Third, I lost my mother to the long, gradual deterioration of Alzheimer's disease, and I worry that I'll go the same way. Research suggests that the brain exercise involved in language learning is an effective deterrent. In other words, I wasn't just glomming on to my children's birth culture. Yet sitting in class, the only person over 35, the only adoptive parent, and one of three white students in a group of eleven, I was aware once again of the risk of cultural appropriation.

Although my memory cells have lost their adhesive power over the years, I've had enough experience with language learning to catch on quickly to grammatical patterns. But I wasn't the best student in the class. That honor fell to a young white entrepreneur who was already fluent in Japanese and looking to expand his business to Korea. As I watched some of the adoptees in class struggle to decipher the *hangul* alphabet and pronounce the words, I felt sad and a little guilty about his and my ease with it. It didn't seem fair that they should have difficulty with the language they were born to or learn to speak it less than fluently. The students who longed to feel at home in Korea or to talk freely with their birth families had so much more at stake than we did.

I recognized one of the students from a fourth-grade class I had served as a parent chaperone at Korean culture camp fifteen years before. I remembered how shy she was back then. She had come to the United States just months before and still wasn't comfortable with English. This time around she was trying to recall the language of her childhood, now repressed in deepest memory. The teacher warned her that her Korean might not resurface, and it apparently didn't. She eventually stopped coming. The attrition rate was alarming. By the end of the second term, only two students remained: the young business-man and I. I felt sad and a little guilty. I wish there were a separate class for adult adoptees that recognizes their emotional investment in the process, urges them on in creative ways, and adapts the lessons to their goals. We never learned, for example, the word *ibyang,* which they need to identify themselves to puzzled Koreans.

When we left for Korea, I took the lesson of that class along in addition to my rudimentary Korean language. I thought it important to practice restraint—not to jump in and attempt a sentence at every opportunity, but to let my daughter and her boyfriend be the interpreters. (In fact, my only lengthy departure from English took place in Danish, a conversation with an adoptee from Denmark who clearly enjoyed relaxing into his native tongue.) It was a pleasure to see Korea through their eyes, to follow their guidance through a country they have come to know on their own terms as their Motherland, but still not quite home.

Restraint should be our watchword in birth family searches as well. While some parents dread the day their child meets that other family, others dream of it as a wondrous moment of resolution. We desire it for ourselves as well as our children. We imagine ourselves welcomed with hugs and tears, treated as kin because of our shared love for this child—no finger-cutting and blood-mixing required. And we long to show the birth parents that their missing child is bright and healthy and happy, to relieve them of worry and shame. Some adoptive parents are so eager to get on with this envisioned reunion that they take up the search before their children are old enough to assent or object, or they ignore the child's indifference or apprehension and figure he'll come around when he sees his parents in the flesh. Deborah Johnson, a Korean American adoptee much in demand as a therapist for internationally and transracially adopted children and their families, cautions that birth family searches should be left to adoptees to take up in their own time. If I could find more information than is in their agency files to put my daughters on the trail of their parents, I wouldn't hesitate to gather it, but I would leave it to them to decide whether and when to follow it. These are *their* families, not mine. I don't want to appropriate for myself what might be the most difficult, emotionally intense, personally meaningful, awesome experience of their lives—other than childbirth, I guess. But if invited, I'll be there in a flash.

Despite all this caution, I'm not recommending a hands-off approach to things Tapodan. Korea is, after all, my "other Motherland." Denmark gave me half my genetic material, but Korea gave me my children. I stay alert to Korea's appearance in the news and gripe about how stereotypically it's portrayed: the madman Kim Jong Il in the north and all those helmeted riot police in the south, with no context to make these images comprehensible. I want to know that context. I can't help but be drawn to anything that reminds me of my own dear daughters. But there's a better way than to become a would-be Korean myself.

Suppose you are a writer, teacher, and critic of poetry, and you learn that Tapoda has a rich lyric tradition worth checking out. You read the few existing translations and become so entranced that you decide to learn Tapodan and find a Tapodan poet to help you render these poems in your own language. Your children couldn't care less about poetry unless it's performed to a hip-hop beat. No matter. You don't need them to vouch for you or to legitimize your interest. *You* are the poet, and your chief interest is poetry.

Or suppose you work in the health professions, and you learn of an exchange program involving Tapodan health personnel. They want hands-on experience in your field, and in return they offer you and your colleagues training in time-honored modes of healing that keep Tapodans remarkably free of the problems your patients encounter. You and the Tapodans share each other's expertise, with no pretense about who you are or which culture has shaped you. The exchange is mutual and respectful, and, again, you don't depend on your children to entitle you to it.

Or maybe you just have a hobbyist's passion for butterflies, and Tapoda is their breeding ground. The point is that you engage with the culture as the person you are, drawing on your own intrinsic interests, with your own ethnicity, your own citizenship. You come out of the experience that same person, but just a little more knowledgeable about, and probably more respectful of, Tapodan culture. Your children will benefit from whatever you learn and whatever avenues of contact you open, but at little or no embarrassment to themselves. You haven't used them as your tickets to this adventure, and you've neither distorted nor romanticized their cultural heritage. You've left them plenty of room to follow their own interests.

Finally, we eager globalists need to remember that *our* multicultural dream is our children's daily reality. They take the measure of global harmony every day in the comments they hear, the glances they catch, the questions they're expected to answer. They may not want to be harbingers or symbols of anything, but just plain human beings. As Kari Ruth puts it, "I guess someone forgot to ask us if we wanted to be America's diversity mascots." Our kids didn't volunteer for our plan to transform the world. We should be satisfied if they simply figure out how to live comfortably in it.

Epilogue

I am only one internationally adoptive parent among hundreds of thousands. My viewpoints are honed by my ethnic origin, my race, my national identity, my religion, my political persuasion, my social class, and a whole lot more. If what I say troubles you, you might seek the counsel of another parent with an outlook more compatible with your own who has also raised adopted children to adulthood. Many of us older parents are ready to listen and to help as stand-in grandparents to the next generations of internationally adoptive families. To find us you will have to leave the comfort of your usual cohort, parents who adopted from the same country—or even the same orphanages and agencies—and in the same span of time.

For about a year, I checked my e-mail almost daily for posts from several Internet listserves I had joined. The greatest number came, understandably, from newer parents soliciting advice from other parents and from adult adoptees. Most of their questions were of the nuts-

and-bolts variety, specific in their intent: "What should I say to my daughter when she tells me she doesn't like her dark skin?" "Should I keep my son's birth name as a middle name even if it has unpleasant connotations in my language?" In answering the questions, the adoptees and older parents often ranged over wide territory—discussions of self-hatred, racial identity, feelings of marginality in both cultures. . . . Then another parent of an elementary-school-age child would send in her (relatively few fathers appear on these lists) advice: "I told my daughter that people spend money in tanning salons to get skin like hers." "We just picked a different name from the same country." Of course this sort of response is natural. Life with children in the house proceeds moment by moment, with the focus held tight.

Yet I recommend that you younger parents from time to time enlarge your focus and ask us older parents open-ended questions. The answers they yield will give you a context for your nuts-and-bolts problems that generates some of its own solutions. Here are some questions to begin with. We older parents could benefit as well from asking them of each other.

- What were your hopes and dreams when you decided to adopt internationally? What expectations did you have? What kind of preparation did you get?

- Were those hopes and dreams fulfilled? Did anything unexpected happen? What were the surprises? Was your preparation helpful?

- Where are your children now? What is your relationship like? Do race and ethnicity figure into it in any way?

- Do you have children-in-law and grandchildren? What are those relationships like? What do the grandchildren understand about the family's adoptive history?

- Have your children been back to their birth country? Have they searched for birth family? Have they found them? Do they have an ongoing relationship with them? Are you involved in this relationship? What has all of this been like for you?

- Were there any times of crisis in your family life? What happened? How did you handle it? What did you learn from it? Would you handle it the same way if you had it to do over?

- Do you have any regrets about the way you raised your children? Is there anything you'd do differently in hindsight?

- What have been the greatest rewards for *you* in this experience? Did they just come, or did you work at them? Do you feel you've been successful as a parent? Have you been changed in any way?

- What do you think about international adoption now? What do your children say about it? Do their feelings about it influence yours? Do you and your children agree?

- What is the single most important piece of advice you would give to someone contemplating international adoption? to someone in the midst of raising a child? to someone whose child has just grown up and left home?

Acknowledgments

Back in the late 1980s, when I set out to write *"Are Those Kids Yours?"*, I located certain adoptive parents, adopted children, and adult adoptees to interview. I asked them to tell me their adoption stories, but I also had a set of questions in mind that I wanted them to answer. It was easy to acknowledge these pseudonymous people for their contributions to the book.

This time I took a different approach. I didn't want my questions to bias the answers or my presence as a writer to inhibit anyone's candor, so I chose to be a passive listener to discussions already under way. I was most curious about how adult adoptees evaluate their upbringings and how parents of adult children reflect on their child-raising experience. I eavesdropped on Internet forums, joined listserves, read books, watched films, and attended conferences. If I were to name all the useful places I traveled in actuality and in cyberspace, this would be a list of resources, not acknowledgments.

Many of the voices that spoke most persuasively I can identify only by screen names. I hope that one huge thank-you to all of you for everything you don't know you taught me will suffice.

There are people closer to home whose names and faces I do know who have not only let me listen, but have also helped me wrestle with tough issues and figure out how to articulate them in prose. Some are members of the indispensable biweekly Moms' Group: Barbara Crosby, Sara Evans, Lonnie Helgeson, Cheryl Rachner Olsen, and Ann Risch. Ginny Jacobson and Linda De Beau Melting, friends through childhood and adolescence, have been my companions on the journey through adoptive parenthood as well. Five of these friends read and discussed a draft of the book along with Maxine Walton of Children's Home Society and Family Services, whose wisdom and compassion I greatly respect, and Jane Jeong Trenka, who wrote the eloquent memoir, *The Language of Blood.* The Ragdale Foundation granted me two weeks of uninterrupted writing, and a chunk of my Minnesota Writers' Career Initiative Grant, administered by the Loft Literary Center, got me to Denmark.

This book would never have come to fruition had Brian Boyd, the publisher of Yeong & Yeong Book Company, not kept a bee buzzing in my bonnet by asking me repeatedly over the years whether I intended to write a sequel to *"Are Those Kids Yours?"* I am grateful for the personal engagement and attention to detail that characterize this small specialty press's relationship with its authors. The intelligence and respectful rigor that adoptive mother and China specialist Amy Klatzkin applied to the task of editing brought my book closer to the ideal of literary perfection that I can't help but strive for.

Finally, I thank my beautiful, loyal, and loving daughters for living this adventure with me and being honest about its complexity. I asked them to read the manuscript and tell me if anything exposed or embarrassed them or just didn't ring true. One read it on the subway to and from work and found nothing objectionable. The other read it in the rooftop garden of her sister's Seoul apartment. When she finished, she looked up, nodded, and said, "Good." That was good enough for me.